THE ANGRY Teenager

Other Books By the Author:

KidThink
Family Cycles
Carry Me Home

THE ANGRY Teenager

◆

DR. WM. LEE CARTER

Thomas Nelson Publishers
Nashville • Atlanta • London • Vancouver

Published in Nashville, Tennessee, by Thomas Nelson, Inc., Publishers, and distributed in Canada by Word Communications, Ltd., Richmond, British Columbia, and in the United Kingdom by Word (UK), Ltd., Milton Keynes, England.

Scripture quotations are from THE NEW KING JAMES VERSION. Copyright © 1979, 1980, 1982, 1990, Thomas Nelson, Inc., Publishers.

Library of Congress Cataloging-in-Publication Data

Carter, Wm. Lee.
   The angry teenager / Wm. Lee Carter.
     p. cm.
   ISBN 0-7852-8002-2 (pbk.)
    1. Anger in adolescence.   2. Anger in adolescence—Case studies.
   3. Child rearing.   I. Title.
   BF724.3.A55C37   1995
   155.5'1247—dc20

                                     94–38176
                                         CIP

Printed in the United States of America

    6 7 — 01 00 99 98 97

Contents

◆

Introduction

◆

I enjoy watching people. My profession certainly encourages it, but I like to do it because it is so entertaining. As I observe all kinds of people, I am curiously intrigued by teenagers. Perhaps they remind me of my own youth. Or, perhaps I want to know as much as I can about the world my children will pass through when they reach adolescence. Whatever the reason, the teenage lifestyle fascinates me.

As I witness groups of teenagers, my mind often wanders into their world. Why do they act, dress, and talk as they do? I notice that so many of them are desperately plodding through this stage of life, trying to rid themselves of that terrible awkward feeling that just won't loosen its grip. A few virtually scoff at their youth with a self-assuredness supposedly reserved for adults. What makes for the differences? What causes one teenager to stumble and tumble through life, while another glides effortlessly?

As I continue to watch teenagers, I inevitably find myself thinking about the homes these young people come from. I often feel confident in predicting which teens are from "good" homes and which are from "bad" homes. But as I dare to look carefully into their eyes, my confidence erodes. Maybe that rough looking kid has parents whose hearts are as good as gold. Or perhaps that quiet, demure teenager has a family life that would make me shudder.

Most of us think of teenagers as unpredictable, and in many ways they are. If we are honest with ourselves, we may admit that we are even afraid of teenagers at times. We fear their behavior, their emotions, their beliefs. Those of us who parent these young people may do so with a certain sense of dread. It seems that our every move is crucial to the teenager's well-being. Could one small slip on our part be the undoing of that teen's entire life?

It is an unavoidable and intimidating fact of parenthood that the interaction between parent and child strongly shapes that child's emotions. Frankly, the parent is in a position to change the path of the young person's journey through life—for better or for worse. Parents must know their teenager so thoroughly that they accurately discern and respond to his needs.

This book deals with adolescence and anger. I am going to explore this emotion *from the teenager's perspective*. Despite its reputation for harming relationships, anger—if properly understood and harnessed—can become a manageable, useful emotional tool.

Teens tell parents a lot about themselves when they release their anger. Listening to the messages beneath that emotion helps parents know how to identify and adjust to the young person's need.

Teenage anger will be treated in a systematic way throughout this book. The first few chapters will define anger as an emotion. Next, I will examine the many faces of anger. Then, factors that can push anger out of control will be identified so that preventative measures can be taken. Finally, I will offer parents ways to step out of harmful family cycles and into patterns that strengthen the teen.

It is my sincere hope that what follows will help both you and your teenager.

Section One

TEENAGE ANGER: WHAT IS IT?

◆

CHAPTER ONE

Hide and Seek with Anger

RECOGNIZING YOUR TEEN'S ANGER

Fifteen-year-old Frank sat glumly in my office. His face looked hard. He was obviously bothered about something. His hair had not been combed, but the look in the youth's eyes suggested he was upset about something far more important than his looks. Two days earlier, he had intentionally hit and injured his thirteen-year-old brother.

Defensively, Frank told me, "I've told my brother a thousand times that he'd better watch himself when he's around me. He never knows when to shut his mouth. He got what was coming to him, but you can't say I hadn't warned him."

"What was coming" was a smashed bottle on the head. The blow opened a wound serious enough to require several stitches. Frank had actually inflicted two wounds—the one to his brother's head and the one to his family's heart. His parents wondered how a teenager could become so angry over insignificant matters. What's more, what could they do to help Frank handle an emotion that had become so difficult to control—anger?

Teenagers commonly experience feelings of anger. All teens know what it means to feel upset because nothing seems to be going right. It is normal for teenagers to feel irritated with their friends or family members. The disappointment an adolescent feels when he meets failure face-to-face is understandable. In fact, I can confidently say that it is *necessary* for a young person to stand up and make his emotions known. But the world can only tolerate a certain amount of anger. There comes a time when anger is not only unnecessary—it is destructive.

A teen with little control over anger has an unclear picture of the hurt he can cause his family and peers. In my counseling practice, I talk regularly with families struggling to control an angry teenager. Parents often openly bare their hurt over family relations that have soured because someone is angry. One emotion repeatedly stands in the way of family unity—anger.

Parents often ask, "Is it normal for my teenager to feel so much anger?" The answer is "Yes." All teens experience this emotion. In fact, I would venture to say an adolescent *should* feel angry. Without this emotional expression, many negative feelings will be bottled up inside the teen and do untold personal and even spiritual harm. But too much of a "good thing" can wreak havoc on a family. Keeping family anger balanced is challenging for any parent!

Anger Has a Bad Reputation

Adults tend to teach their children that anger is wrong. Have you ever said to your child, "You are not allowed to talk to me in that angry tone of voice"? I have. More than likely, we all have sent the message to our children that "bad" people get angry. "Good" people get rid of their anger.

An insightful fourteen-year-old girl once said to me, "My mother told me the other day that she is surprised at how angry I get when she tells me I can't have everything my way. While she was talking to me her voice got louder and louder and her face became red. She said, 'Haven't I told you that nobody will respect you if you keep losing your temper the way you do? You've got to get rid of that habit!' You should have seen how mad my mom was when she told me that I need to quit being so angry!" The girl smiled at the irony of her mother's behavior.

Merely telling our teens to quit being angry doesn't do much good. We need to teach them how to use this emotion constructively.

Not only will the teen profit from learning "anger control," the whole family will benefit. Throughout this book, I will maintain that anger is not a "bad" emotion. It only becomes bad when it is misused. The psalmist warns us, "Be angry, and do not sin" (Ps. 4:4). Implied is the message that anger does not have to be sinful, but can be useful. Our first task as parents is to understand what this emotion is and what it is not so our teaching will be productive.

Anger Is Not Supposed to Be . . .

Sometimes a concept is best described by what it is *not*. We all have preconceived ideas about what anger is, so the following ideas of what anger *is not* may surprise you:

- *Anger is not supposed to "pound home" a point.* When Frank felt it necessary to hit his younger brother with a bottle to make a point, he used anger to literally force attention to his message. This use of anger shows an unwillingness to consider alternative points of view. The wayward goal of angry communication is not to interact meaningfully, but to simply shove an opinion on someone else, no matter what the cost.
- *Anger is not supposed to condemn.* We will inevitably have conflicting opinions with others. Teens are often *too* certain that they know what is right, a dogmatic decision that leaves no room for others' ideas. Condemning anger censures those who differ. The angry message is: *"I'm right and you're wrong!"*
- *Anger is not supposed to isolate.* As a group of teenagers talked candidly about anger, one girl laughed as she blurted out, "Hey, at least everybody leaves me alone when I'm mad!" Her peers laughed, too, but most of them knew this girl was very lonely. The fear that drove her anger isolated her from others. The verbal jabs of an angry teen may intimidate others and drive them away. Though an angry teen may enjoy a few moments of solitude, the loneliness that accompanies overworked

anger is painful. Many teens complain about feeling left out, yet do not realize that their pessimistic attitudes only make fulfilling relationships harder to find.

- *Anger is not supposed to rule others.* Teenagers will quickly tell you that they enjoy being "spoiled." It feels good to know that others will cater to even their smallest needs. Anger, however, may cause a teen to *demand* treatment reserved only for fairy-tale kings and queens. One teenager told a well-adjusted friend, "My Dad wouldn't buy me another tank of gas. He says one tank a week is plenty. What's his problem, anyway? Since when does he know how much driving around I have to do?" When the friend said he would gladly receive one tank of gas per week, the angry teen wheeled away in disgust. His anger had convinced him that life owed him a full tank of favors!

- *Anger is not supposed to harden.* Our world sends teens a garbled message of what it takes to cope with life's realities. Many angry teens confuse being cooperative with being a "doormat." They use angry facades to appear strong against those who take advantage of weaklings. Countless teens in serious trouble melt when they come into contact with just one person who expresses care and concern. Many of these "bad" kids will admit that their angry exterior is just a way of putting bandages on their emotional wounds.

- *Anger is not supposed to intimidate.* From an early age, children are encouraged to cooperate with others. Time and experience teach young people, however, that angry expressions can make people jump into action. Shouting, "shooting daggers" with cold eyes, or telling hurtful secrets puts teens in control over others. Teens may enjoy the power surge that accompanies their intimidation, but the lingering results can ruin relationships. Tension abounds in homes where a teen's angry emotions run amuck.

- *Anger is not supposed to blind.* One frustrated parent said of her angry daughter, "Can't she see what she is doing to herself? She is constantly making enemies because of the way she treats people. You'd think she would realize this and tone her emotions down just a little bit." An unfortunate side effect of unbridled anger is its short-sighted view of life. As if he is strolling around blindfolded, an angry teenager fails to see his most obvious weaknesses. What's more, the teen will often refuse to acknowledge the need to change.

How Parents Can Help Angry Teens

I believe parents are in a position to give an adolescent the leadership that helps them make wise choices. Parents cannot force a teenager to think or act in a specific way. Any parent who has tried to force change on an angry teen can testify to the negative results of trying to overpower a teenager. But parents *can* make a difference in a teenager's understanding of anger.

Angry behavior can be rewarding to a teenager. A parent's response can reduce that reward. The young person may abuse his anger or use it as a manipulation tool. A parent can blunt those manipulative and wounding effects of anger. Anger can send relationships crashing. It can claim revenge on others. Ultimately, it can become a chosen lifestyle. An understanding parent can loosen anger's grip on a teenager.

Too frequently parents try to force help on young people. We tell them exactly what they need to know to make their life better. Like a boomerang, these efforts come back to strike us. Note the following ways parents unsuccessfully try to help a young person struggling with anger:

- We take away prized possessions, hoping to coerce the adolescent to cooperate.

7

- We ground the young person so he will have time to think about constructive ways to handle his or her emotions.
- We use physical force to pressure the young person to conform to reasonable standards.
- We induce guilt in the teen in the hope that repentance will follow.
- We withhold tenderness and affection so the young person will respect our emotions.
- We force adolescents to sit through lectures and sermons so we can fill them with our wisdom and knowledge.

This book will encourage you to view anger as your teenager experiences it. Parents can be most helpful when they understand their child completely. Angry teens often hurl the accusation, "You just don't understand me!" as a rationale for their behavior. When parents take away that complaint, healing can begin.

As he was told of his daughter's need for understanding, one father said to me, "If I tell her I understand, she'll think I agree with her. Nothing could be farther from the truth. I *don't* agree!" As this man began to realize that understanding and agreement are not synonyms, he learned how to give understanding to his daughter without agreeing with her. Teenagers know their parents well enough to know when there is agreement and when there is not. They also know when understanding is present and when it is not.

This book is intended to equip you with the knowledge and skills to help you guide your adolescent through the tidal wave of emotions that characterize the teenage years. It is not enough to simply love your child so much that he or she will glide into adulthood. Of course, love is critical, as are the teen's needs for understanding, patience, communication, and positive direction. But I believe that coupling the natural love you already feel for your child with a knowledge of the world around him is the best step toward really helping your teenager.

In the following pages, you may be surprised at the complexity of the emotion of anger. Its many faces often make it difficult to recognize and manage. I encourage you to follow the guidelines offered, even if it means a marked departure from your normal way of responding to your teen. My goal is to help you make this oft-misunderstood emotion your teen's ally.

◆

CHAPTER TWO

How Does Your Teenager Rate?

DETERMINING HOW PREVALENT AN ISSUE ANGER IS IN YOUR FAMILY

Have you ever tried to characterize your teenager's anger? I confess that I have. My wife, Julie, and I talk to one another about our frustrations with our three daughters. More than once I have made a comment to Julie that sounds something like this: "I can't believe she just said that! That is one stubborn girl. It doesn't take anything at all to make her mad. We'd better stay away from her for a while. There's no telling what she might say if we try to talk to her when she's in one of *those* moods."

Or how about this one? Julie might say, "Lee, you're going to have to look after the girls tonight. My nerves are about shot. Everything I've said to them today has been taken the wrong way. They're mad at me and I'm mad at them, so I think it's best that we stay out of each others' way for a while. I'm not interested in getting into any more fights. You take the wheel!" Sound familiar?

Let me add that my children are fully aware that their dad is a psychologist—a child psychologist at that. Nonetheless, they came into the world garnished with the same emotions as all other children. While my role at the office is to guide other families toward fulfilling relationships, I assume the parental role once I walk through the arches of our front door. Julie and I have the responsibility to lead our children to a healthy understanding of themselves in the hope that they will become all God intends them to be. Our three daughters feel the same emotional surges as all red-blooded children.

Likewise, I get worked up over my children's antics as any other parent would. I work daily to achieve the same things I will suggest in this book. Understanding teenagers is hard work, and I know it!

To help characterize teen anger, I have developed a brief test for you. The only preparation is to be familiar with your teenage child and to know how he tends to express his feelings through words and actions.

Listed below is a series of statements that relate to the way adolescents may express anger inappropriately. Read each item and answer yes or no as it applies to your teenager most of the time. If you have more than one adolescent in your house, rate each one separately. (You have permission to make extra copies for personal use of these pages.) Ready?

My teenager . . .

1.	becomes excited or upset every few days	yes	no
2.	loses his cool when he is told "No"	yes	no
3.	is easily influenced by negative peers	yes	no
4.	seems to frequently take advantage of others	yes	no
5.	throws what I would call a temper tantrum when he is upset	yes	no
6.	acts in ways to "get even" with me or others	yes	no
7.	does things without concern for what might happen next	yes	nc
8.	fights back harder when punished	yes	no
9.	takes risks that could result in serious harm to himself or others	yes	no
10.	becomes destructive of property when upset	yes	no
11.	complains that no one cares about him	yes	no
12.	says things to suggest he feels sorry for himself	yes	no
13.	accuses me of not understanding him	yes	no
14.	gets so touchy I can't even reason with him	yes	no

15. becomes dramatic and showy when upset   yes   no
16. brings up irrelevant information he knows I am sensitive about   yes   no
17. often complains about what will happen to him   yes   no
18. refuses to talk to me for a long time when angry   yes   no
19. says things such as, "I wish I'd never been born"   yes   no
20. puts himself down more than I think is healthy   yes   no
21. lies around the house doing virtually nothing   yes   no
22. often wears a frown or sad expression   yes   no
23. sleeps too much or too little   yes   no
24. has no appetite or eats too much   yes   no
25. complains often of feeling bored   yes   no
26. has a low self-esteem   yes   no
27. is easily irritated by the little things other people do   yes   no
28. becomes discouraged rather easily   yes   no
29. seems less sure of himself than his friends do   yes   no
30. complains that he is not appreciated by others   yes   no

As you look at how you have just rated your teenager, it will help you to evaluate your responses by examining them as follows:

- Items 1–10 deal with the way your teenager *behaves* when upset. Understanding the action of an angry teenager allows a parent to know what is inside his heart. Teenagers often show family members their anger by the way they act toward others, even those who have their best interest at heart. Or, a teen may make a statement about his feelings by the peer group he associates with, or by his behavior when he is with that group. As we will learn, teenagers tell us a lot about themselves through their behavior. Emotions play a large role in the choices a young person makes as he attempts to deal openly with his feelings.

13

If you responded yes to five or more of the items numbered 1 through 10, it will be important to pay close attention to your teenager's behavior. He is trying to tell you something about his anger.

- Items 11–20 are concerned with how your teenager *communicates* his feelings to you. Some teens talk loudly and freely about what they think is wrong, but have dim insight into the effect of their own behavior. Others cling to their angry feelings, making you guess at what they really feel. Some make statements that practically beg for sympathy and understanding. Helping a teen effectively communicate angry feelings is one of the greatest ways a parent can boost a struggling young person. If you responded yes to five or more of the items numbered 11 through 20, your teenager is probably trying to tell you his feelings, but does not know how to appropriately communicate them.

- The items numbered 21–30 are concerned with your teenager's *emotional well-being*. A teenager who constantly wrestles with anger can take a real emotional beating as he tries to corral this formidable emotion. When an emotion as potent as anger chokes a young person, the result can be depression, diminished feelings of self-worth, or a sense of despair. Your awareness of your child's communication failures may be the starting point for controlling his anger. If you responded yes to five or more items numbered 21 through 30, your teenager may be carrying an emotional burden that needs to be lightened. He needs your helping hand in trimming away excess anger.

Now that you have some understanding of your teenager's characteristic way of dealing with anger, let's veer in a different direction. I would like you to step outside yourself for just a moment and be bold enough to see yourself the way your teenager sees you. If you feel especially brave, ask your teenager to rate you on the same set of items and compare responses. The following rating scale deals with the way *you* respond to your own anger as it relates to your adolescent child. As with the first rating scale, read each item and rate yourself by responding yes or no to each one. Be completely honest. You might encourage your spouse to respond to this questionnaire after you have. You will learn a lot about the role anger plays in your family. (You have permission to make extra copies for personal use of these pages.)

I . . .

1.	frequently get hooked into power struggles	yes	no
2.	dole out harsh punishment for misconduct	yes	no
3.	have been known to get right in my teenager's face as I tell him what he did wrong	yes	no
4.	do what I can to shame my child when I'm angry	yes	no
5.	can be animated when upset	yes	no
6.	attack others with sarcasm or verbal threats	yes	no
7.	slam doors or throw things when I am frustrated	yes	no
8.	like to have the last word in an argument	yes	no
9.	withdraw and refuse to talk when upset	yes	no
10.	demand that my children show respect	yes	no
11.	am quicker to point out faults than I am to offer encouragement	yes	no
12.	tend to bring up the past in conversations	yes	no
13.	find myself thinking of what I will say next while others talk to me	yes	no
14.	often give long lectures	yes	no
15.	try to motivate through the use of criticism	yes	no
16.	find it hard to see others' point of view	yes	no
17.	have a hard time walking away from arguments	yes	no

18. make frequent predictions about what will happen if better choices are not made   yes   no
19. wish my family would just see things as I do   yes   no
20. don't like to verbalize my feelings   yes   no
21. feel discouraged in my role as a parent   yes   no
22. have negative expectations for my family   yes   no
23. feel unappreciated in my own home   yes   no
24. am so overwhelmed I sometimes want to give
up   yes   no
25. experience a lot of guilt for my teen's behavior   yes   no
26. find myself with no energy to fight any longer   yes   no
27. have a hard time making decisions these days   yes   no
28. think that maybe I'm being punished   yes   no
29. receive limited satisfaction from my family life   yes   no
30. worry so much that I literally feel sick   yes   no

As in the first list, items 1 through 10 help you identify *behaviors* you may show that could contribute to an angry mood in the home. Those numbered 11 through 20 deal with the typical ways you *communicate* with your family. The final ten items have to do with the effects of your own *emotional* status as it relates to family relationships. Responding yes to five or more items within each of these groups may raise a red flag of caution.

By identifying the behaviors, communication patterns, and emotional expressions you could work to shore up, your teen will benefit as you come to grips with that bewildering emotion of anger. And what's more, you will also experience satisfaction in the form of improved family relationships.

Let me add a word of both warning and hope. Parents may assume strong feelings of guilt over the emotions and behaviors displayed by their children. Stay away from that trap. In every family, each person is only responsible for playing out his own role as the family story unfolds. No one family member can assume all the responsibility for what another family member will choose to do.

At the same time, each family member must depend on the others before success in relationships is realized. When the parent assumes the role of leadership, teenagers are usually quick to respond positively when healthy behavior is modeled, communication is open, and emotions are balanced. Thus, while the parent need not assume all the burden for the ills of the family, it is possible to use the parental leadership position as a powerful tool that shapes the emotion of anger into one that can help, rather than harm, the family.

◆

CHAPTER THREE

This Is How I Feel about Myself!

HOW ANGER IMPACTS A TEEN'S SELF-ESTEEM

Oh yeah, I get angry alright. My boyfriend will tell you that. Just ask him what happens when he gets me mad. I'm not the nicest person to be around when I'm mad. He'll tell you that!" The teenaged girl faked a laugh as she talked. An odd, deceiving shroud surrounded her laughter. It hurt to look into her eyes. She seemed proud to be able to emotionally cut others to the bone. She talked bluntly, even heartlessly, about her anger.

"I can cut people to shreds when I'm mad," the girl, Sheila, boasted. "I even surprise myself with some of the things I say."

"No doubt you surprise others, too, with your cutting remarks," I responded. Sheila seemed willing to look at herself objectively.

The conversation continued. Sheila slowly became more serious. She drew a deep breath and mumbled, "The other day I told my mother that she was the absolute worst person in the world." Silently the girl paused a brief moment before blurting out, "And sometimes she is! She can make me madder than almost anybody else I know. I told her I hated her." That statement made, she quietly looked downward.

I tried to think as Sheila thought. "You've probably had more arguments with your mother than you would like. Arguing with boyfriends and parents all the time can wear you out."

Sheila looked up. Her face ached with pain, replacing the hard, carefree attitude she had shown moments earlier. "Do you know what it's like to feel that you're never going to get along with anyone?"

"I can only imagine that it must hurt."

"Uh hmm. It does." Sheila's voice trailed off again. A brief moment later she added, "Sometimes I hate life."

"You know, Sheila, when we find ourselves fighting with other people all the time, we must struggle to find anything good about life. I imagine you even find it hard to think of anything good about yourself too."

"That's the truth," she muttered.

Slightly smiling, I asked Sheila, "What *do* you think about yourself?"

"I don't know," shrugged Sheila.

"Tough question, wasn't it?"

"Yeah. Well, I can tell you this. When I think of myself, it's not always real good. I've done a lot of bad things. I've made a lot of people mad. In fact I stay mad most of the time."

"When you think about yourself, you can't get away from the word 'anger.' Right?"

"Yeah. You're probably right. I'm angry a lot of the time."

I knew then that Sheila was honestly trying to understand herself.

Anger Can Be a Descriptive Term

Adolescents face the chore of recognizing their personal strengths and weaknesses. Simply getting a teenager to do that is a tough challenge. Just ask anyone who has lived with one! Many teenagers are like Sheila. They harbor strong feelings of anger, letting it show through their behavior. Their frequent run-ins with others blind them to a better way of life. They are unsure whether their anger is a help or a hindrance. At times anger offers a needed defense against potential personal harm. At other times it tears relationships apart. Confusion is the result.

Angry teens often use common statements to define themselves. Some of them include:

- *It's common to feel tense inside.*
- *Try as I may to hold my feelings in, they just burst out.*
- *Others tell me I argue too much.*
- *I have a guilty conscience about the things I think and do.*
- *I admit I think other people are better than I am.*
- *I am critical of others, though I keep my thoughts to myself.*
- *My relationships with others are stormy.*
- *Others would probably say I am "bad."*
- *I get upset easily when I do what I know I shouldn't do.*
- *When I am angry, I don't care what I do, even if it is wrong.*
- *I have a hard time making myself do things I don't want to do.*
- *People complain that I am moody.*

Each of the above statements describes anger. A teenager who makes such comments has a problem with anger. Anger, in fact, becomes a defining characteristic of the teen. It can even dominate his self-esteem.

The Beginnings of an Angry Self-Esteem

Let's remember that anger is not inherently a bad emotion. All of us have experienced anger at various points in our lives. Feeling angry is as basic to human life as feeling hungry, or tired, or satisfied, or afraid. It is common to all of us. Drift back in time to when your teenager was a baby. Even an infant shows anger when he feels ignored, or hurt, or hungry. An infant's anger can result from an unmet need or physical discomfort. Innocently, the baby is asking for relief from tension.

As an infant grows through childhood into adolescence and then adulthood, anger becomes personalized. Circumstances or events that upset one young person do not phase another. The uniqueness of each child's personality accounts for much of this difference. Additionally, the individual's life experiences give shape to anger. A child learns through his experiences how this emotion fills a need.

A child learns to express anger before she can even walk or talk. Parents are often surprised to discover how observant an infant can be. This young child can accurately detect a foul mood or uncomfortable feeling in an adult caretaker. An infant notices changes in daily routine. A parent's, or even sibling's, tension can be felt by the infant.

Surprisingly, an infant may identify moods even more accurately than an adult. The child's inability to deny the obvious contributes to his clear, though naive, perception. He does not make excuses or try to deceive others. An infant does not take sides in an argument or hold grudges. In their innocence, these young children absorb all their world has to offer as they learn to define themselves.

To return to Sheila's illustration, we can see anger's role in her self-esteem development. According to her mother, Sheila was always a little different from her brother. The mother once commented, "I thought boys were supposed to be naturally more aggressive than girls, but it's not that way in our family. Sheila has always been more aggressive than her younger brother." Her inborn temperament led her to be more easily irritated than most children.

By the time she was only one year old, Sheila built quite a reputation for her temper tantrums. At bedtime, she demanded absolute silence. Her mother and dad wearily took turns softly bouncing her on a pillow, hoping she would quickly fall asleep, but she seldom did. Relatives accused the parents of coddling the girl and warned that she would become spoiled. Sheila's parents defensively challenged anyone to come up with a better method of avoiding her bedtime tantrums.

Throughout her childhood, Sheila absorbed others' reactions into her self-concept. She learned that her anger aggravated her family and used it to manipulate them. She could protest unfavorable decisions and often have them overturned. She learned to "pay back" her challengers by refusing to cooperate or by withholding information.

Sheila's forceful temperament was not the cause of all the family conflict, however. Her parents fought regularly over petty matters. Her father concluded he had married the wrong woman and spent increasing amounts of time away from home. He thought he could be happier away from his chaotic, argumentative home.

Again, Sheila observed and interpreted the events of her world. She mistakenly assumed that she was the root cause of her parents' disagreements. Years later her mother told her, "Sheila, I don't want you to think that you were the cause of my and Dad's marital problems. Our fights had nothing to do with you."

Separately, however, Sheila mused, *I know my parents have told me not to blame myself for all of our family's troubles, but what am I supposed to think? I can hear them when they argue. My name gets mentioned a whole lot more often than my brother's. How can they say I'm not the cause of their problems when they're constantly fighting over me?*

A combination of factors shaped Sheila's progression into an angry adolescent. Not only did she have a strong disposition, she tested the limits of her world and then interpreted what she had seen. At various times she showed others what she had concluded about herself through the statements she made. These included:

- *I am difficult to get along with.*
- *People often misinterpret my actions.*
- *I ruin others' relationships.*
- *Other people are happier than I am.*
- *It's hard for my family to really love me.*
- *I don't get the emotional support I need from others.*
- *My chances for a happy life are pretty slim.*

These thoughts formed Sheila's self-concept. Thus, in answer to the question, "What do you *really* think about yourself?" she could only respond according to a warped self-concept. Anger dominated her thinking. When someone told Sheila that this emotion dominated her opinion of herself, she asked herself, *"Is it correct for me to feel the way I do about myself?"* It was then possible for her to shape a more positive self-concept.

Sheila's development into an angry teenager illustrates how young people can come to negative conclusions about their personal value. By helping the teen cope with angry feelings, a parent can positively penetrate the teen's sense of worth. Understanding that anger can become intertwined in the teen's self-esteem is a starting point. Looking beyond anger at other basic needs of the child is the second step.

Teens Don't Like a Lot of Things

To say that teenagers do not like a lot of things about life is certainly an understatement. One parent expressed this thought when talking of her teenaged son: "I used to think my son liked himself and had a good self-concept. But since entering adolescence, he always seems to have something negative to say. I'm not sure he even likes himself anymore."

Adolescence marks an awkward time when young people are trying to figure out how to act like grown-ups. A young child lacks the intellectual ability to consider the many pressures confronting him. But the young teen, with his adult-like reasoning ability, may be overwhelmed by life's demands. It is common for teens, especially young ones, to show a drop in self-esteem. Many teens stumble before learning to gracefully glide through this stage of life.

Consider the following scenarios highlighting some of the adjustments required of the young teen:

- Fourteen-year-old Andy had never really thought about having a girlfriend. Feeling clumsy around girls, he simply ignored them. But he was struck by a swelling, funny feeling about a girl in his English class. She seemed different from the other girls. Wanting to build a friendship with her, he mustered the courage to sit with her one day during lunchtime. Not only did he get tongue-tied, he also got ribbed mercilessly by his friends.

- Marie went on an overnight trip with a church group. Late in the night several older girls announced their plan to sneak out of their rooms in search of excitement in a nearby town. Marie was pressured to go along with them, despite her discomfort. When the adult chaperone caught the girls, Marie had to face the same consequences as her older friends. She was upset with her friends for leading her into trouble.

- Lane had been raised in a conservative home. The high school experience overwhelmed him. Simply put, he was unprepared for the fast-paced demands of his age group. Discomfort plagued him. He wanted to feel the thrill of being a teenager, but knew his parents would frown on his new peer group. He constantly struggled to make the right choice.

- Tricia's friends seemed to know so much more about sex than she did. As her girlfriends talked about these things, she was simultaneously plagued by curiosity and guilt. She did not want to question her parents for fear that they might be upset with her for thinking about sex. But, she certainly did not want to look to her friends for answers. She knew she would become the laughing stock of her peer group if she admitted her ignorance on the subject.

It's no wonder anger weaves its way into the self-concept of many teenagers. Faced with previously unknown dilemmas, the teen may experience internal emotions he can neither explain nor contain. Ironically, few adults understand these same dilemmas! Teens search for answers to baffling teenage problems, just like their parents.

Make Your Teen's World Comfortable

Sheila's parents focused on making their home a more comfortable place. One root cause of Sheila's self-concept was her uncertainty about family relationships. Their home atmosphere did not assure her of her importance as a person. Her description of herself as an angry teenager highlighted the need to redirect her negative thoughts.

It is impossible to talk an angry teen out of her emotions. Yet, it *is* possible to alter the mood of the home to encourage the teen to change how she interprets her emotions. A parent's change frees a teen to conclude that she is not the negative person she thought she was. Ways Sheila's parents attempted to alter their home environment included:

- listening more intently to the underlying emotions beneath Sheila's angry outbursts
- paying closer attention to how they handled disagreements over Sheila
- allowing Sheila to voice her thoughts completely before offering their advice or opinions
- complimenting Sheila when she resolved conflicts in a relatively calm manner
- allowing her to elaborate on her thoughts before jumping to conclusions about what she actually meant
- openly expressing affection toward Sheila
- taking an interest in the things that were important to Sheila

A young person's self-esteem takes years to fully develop. Parents of teens are often frustrated at the teen's relatively slow reaction to their changes. Even after seeing some positive changes in her family, Sheila remarked with a sense of doubt, "Yeah, I've noticed that they're trying to change." Her explanation for her skepticism was, "I'm not too sure if they can keep it up. They've acted nice to me before, but we somehow seem to wind up back at the same old place—always arguing about stupid things that don't really matter."

One of the reasons for Sheila's anger centered around the inconsistency in her family relationships. Just as it had taken time to conclude that her life had limited value, it took time to reverse that negative trend in her thinking. The warm acceptance of an angry teen sends the message, "You are an important person, full of value." Consistency over time makes a believer of a doubting young person.

CHAPTER FOUR

◆

Let Me Tell You What's on My Mind!

ANGER IS A COMMUNICATION DEVICE

Anger has numerous functions. At times, anger is the response a young person makes to his world. An angry teen may be showing what he has learned in frequent family conflicts. In other cases, angry expressions may represent the teen's frustration over unmet needs for recognition or affection. Or, an angry teen may be exhibiting just how self-centered he has become.

One common denominator of all angry expressions is that they are communication tools. As teenagers expose their anger, all of them hope to convey a message. A great irony of anger is that the more forceful its expression, the less effective its message.

CASE STUDY: *Ben's Anger Makes a Point*

Ben was thirteen when he first began to show signs of rebellion. His perplexed parents noted, "We recognized a distinct change in our son when he was in the eighth grade. We don't know if it was his peer group pushing him into such negative behavior, or if adolescence just hit him the wrong way. We *do* know that in the last three years we have seen our son transform from a decent young man to one we can hardly tolerate."

Once, Ben had defied his father when asked to mow the grass before making plans to spend the night with a friend. In the past, Ben might have grumbled and complained, but he would have obeyed his father. Now older and more brazen, he simply refused to do as his father requested.

As a fifteen-year-old, Ben went to the mall one Friday evening with a friend, but did not come home until well past midnight. His worried parents were both furious and relieved when he finally dragged through the door. His only explanation was, "Martin wanted me to go with him to Todd's house, so I did." When his parents chastised his poor judgment, he blew up, complaining that none of his friend's parents were as strict as his.

By the time Ben was sixteen he seemed consumed with anger. He seldom spoke to family members except to grunt a complaint or negative comment. When given direct advice or guidance by his parents, he would either shout his disapproval or walk out in silent protest. There seemed to be no middle ground in the way he expressed his feelings.

In my office Ben seemed different from the picture his parents had painted of him. A fairly quiet young man, he was cordial and polite and certainly not disagreeable. After gaining his confidence I said, "Ben, something doesn't seem right to me. You've heard how your parents describe you. They say you blow up easily over little things. They also say you simply refuse to talk because you're so mad. Yet, to me you look like a normal teenaged boy. What causes the difference?"

Ben laughed, "It drives my parents crazy when I act nice to other people!"

"You mean you act polite toward others, but you're angry at home just to drive your parents crazy?" I asked. Ben's comment did not make sense.

Ben smiled as if he had a secret to tell. "No, that's not why I act like that. I act angry at home because I *am* angry. I don't think they understand that. I'm not kidding when I tell my parents I'm mad about something."

Ben was being honest. I wanted to hear more. "Oh, I'm sure

your parents realize you're not kidding. Maybe you're making such a strong statement that they can't hear what you're saying."

"What do you mean? You think I'm not getting my message across strong enough?" Ben almost laughed at my suggestion. I could not help but laugh with him.

"It's not that you're not stating your feelings strongly enough. I've gotten the idea that you let everybody know exactly how you feel!" With that comment, Ben looked more closely at himself. I continued, "In fact, maybe that's the problem. You are trying so hard to communicate that you're upset, and your parents are focusing on keeping your anger from getting out of hand. When they do that, they don't hear what you'd really like to say to them." I could tell that he was thinking hard now.

I asked Ben to name some of the messages he would like to communicate to his parents through his anger. He came up with a long list. It included:

- *I wonder how much I count in this family.*
- *It bothers me a great deal when I am criticized.*
- *I need to convince myself that I can do what others want me to do.*
- *I sometimes feel that others owe me more than I have been given.*
- *I feel guilty when others blame me for the problems I create.*
- *I don't think people know what it's like to be me.*
- *I want to learn for myself what my strengths and weaknesses are.*
- *I have questions about the reasons you believe the things you believe.*
- *People look at my bad side instead of my good side.*

After reviewing this list, I asked Ben, "I suspect you know what your parents' responses to these statements would be, don't you?"

"Oh yeah, I know exactly what they think about everything I do," he responded, without hesitation.

"You know, it's odd, Ben, that your parents know you so well and you know them inside-out too. Yet, for you to communicate your thoughts to them, you feel you need to angrily force them out." Ben nodded with agreement at the irony of his communication style with his parents Now we were getting somewhere.

Anger Can Make a Teen Look Bad

Teenagers often remark that they feel rather foolish after they look honestly at the way they express their feelings. In our conversations, Ben told of a time when he defied a household rule by smuggling cigarettes into his bedroom. Rather than obey his parents' simple request to remove the cigarettes from the house (he was not even asked to throw them away), he defiantly lit one up a few minutes later. Although he dared not make this confession to his parents, he conceded to me with a chuckle, "That probably wasn't the smartest thing I ever did."

Yet when he further explained his behavior, lighting the cigarette made a little more sense, albeit unwise: "I just wanted my parents to treat me with a little respect."

"You mean, the way they told you to get rid of your cigarettes offended you?"

"Well, kinda. My dad went into this spiel about how nasty cigarettes are and how they're bad for you and how no son of his was going to smoke them if he had anything to do with it."

"So you weren't bothered so badly because your dad told you to remove the cigarettes, but because he made you feel like you didn't know that smoking is bad for your health."

"Yeah, I know that. He didn't have to tell me."

"When you lit the cigarette, then, you intended to send your dad a message . . ."

Ben completed the thought, "Don't treat me like a little kid. I'm sixteen years old!"

Ben had communicated his feelings with defiance. While it is hard to agree with the way he broadcast his emotions, his need was valid. He was guilty of violating a house rule. That experience alone can create a certain degree of humility. A baseball player friend once told of how humiliating it was to trudge to the dugout after being caught trying to steal a base. In front of thousands of people, he had to admit he had failed.

While most teen rule violations are not witnessed by throngs of people, an embarrassed teenager will often recoil in anger. To him it seems he has failed in front of the entire world. His hope is to salvage something good from a bad situation. Unfortunately, in trying to make something positive out of a negative, the young person usually makes matters worse. In the process, he diminishes the credibility of his intended communication.

Listen as Anger Talks

With Ben's permission, his parents looked over the list of messages he and I had drawn up to explain his anger toward their leadership. They looked over the list pensively. Mr. Talbot commented, "You know, when I read these messages, I can see how Ben would think these things. I don't agree with everything he says, because I think we aren't as hard on him as he makes us out to be. But I can just hear Ben talking as I read this list. We've heard these complaints in one form or fashion many times."

Wanting to understand her son, Mrs. Talbot asked, "How do we react to Ben when he so blatantly throws his anger at us? Of course we want to make him feel understood, but when he's angry, it's hard to get anything across to him—even if we're trying to be positive!"

We must listen to what a teen's anger says. Understanding his emotions can soften the urge to overpower him with punishment or arguments. When a teenager expresses his emotions, he is often saying one of the following statements.

- *"Hey, somebody take note of my needs!"* Through overstatement, he is asking to be treated fairly. Angry teenagers often feel ignored or unappreciated.

33

- *"I feel embarrassed by the mistakes I've made."* To recoup his lost dignity, the teen may hide embarrassment with anger.
- *"My world is slipping away from my control!"* Once a teenager has tasted independence, it is hard to give up that feeling of power.
- *"I need to be convinced that I can make decisions."* When a teen has been challenged, even appropriately, for making an unwise choice, he needs reassurance that he is the capable person he is trying to become.
- *"I want to learn all about life—right now!"* Adolescence opens the young person to a world of new personal experiences and opportunities. The impatient teen explodes when someone tries to slow him down.

Stay Away from Short-Term Cures

Looking at these hidden messages beneath teenage anger, we cannot argue their validity. But, we must go back to Mrs. Talbot's question of how to respond to her son's defiance. One of the most useful guidelines in handling teen anger is to avoid trying to purge all anger from the teen at once. A common knee-jerk reaction to defiant behavior is to try to overpower the rebellious youth. Mr. Talbot voiced what most parents feel when they have been angrily opposed by a child, "When Ben had the nerve to smoke in the house right after I had told him to get rid of his cigarettes, I wanted to take away every privilege he had. I wanted to take everything he owns and throw it in a trash dumpster. Maybe that would have taught him a good lesson!"

Fortunately, Mr. Talbot had not followed his urges. To have done so would have added fuel to an already hot fire within Ben. Of course, Ben's behavior required his parents to supervise him more closely. They hoped to prevent him from making further costly mistakes. Ben's poor judgment called for closer monitoring than a more responsible young person would require. Yet, other parental responses were needed beyond the need to closely guard their son from his own mistakes.

Many parents have disciplined a teen hoping to teach a valuable lesson, only to watch that teen blow even more anger. Adults can let their anger get tangled up in their words just as young people do. Messages need to be sent in ways the teen understands.

Here are some guidelines for communicating with an angry teenager:

- *Defuse a potentially explosive situation* between yourself and your teen by walking away from likely confrontations. A teenager who does not have a verbal sparring partner is more likely to let "hot" emotions pass. In a case like Ben's, it is sometimes better to walk away from a certain verbal slugfest. His defiance is his way of asking for a fight he knows he can win. By trying to overpower him, the parent may win the battle, but lose the war. A teenager is fully aware of his parents' frustration tolerance.

- *Focus attention on things you can control,* specifically your own emotional reaction. Viewing the teen's behavior objectively allows you to "hear" the hidden messages the young person is trying to send to you. If you feel your defiant teen is asking for greater independence, give him independence in things he is likely to handle appropriately. If he is stating feelings of frustration over a weak self-image, make efforts to boost his worth through positive interaction. One stark reality of dealing with an angry teenager is that he cannot be *forced* to do what he has made up his mind not to do. Your teen knows this and willingly takes advantage of situations that give him a competitive edge. But the good news is that an emotionally-controlled parent can influence him in the right direction.

- *Talk with your teen* after his intense emotions have passed. A frequent mistake we parents make in dealing with an angry teen is to vent our emotions when a crisis is in progress. Our own emotions may be as intense as the teen's. To release our emotions at their peak will likely escalate the tension. By waiting until the intensity of the moment has died down, healing communication is more probable.

- *Let your actions speak louder* than your words. This age-old adage is well worn but true. An angry parent may make threats, accusations, or predictions in an angry tone of voice hoping to get through to an irresponsible young person. Instead of listening to the words of the adult, though, the teen will take note of how he caused the parent to go into emotional orbit. Ignoring his parent's words, he will take advantage of the chance to prey on the adult's emotions.

- *Take an inventory* of your relationship with your teenager. Remember, through his anger a teenager may be stating that he is unsure of himself. The irony of this is that he may be so angry that the parent ignores his real need. Spending quality time with your teenager can take the edge off his anger.

CHAPTER FIVE

◆

Caught in a Trap

HOW A TEEN CAN BE VICTIMIZED BY ANGER

A thirteen-year-old girl slumped lifelessly in her chair. Her face was drawn—her eyebrows turned in and mouth tightly pursed. Her dirty blonde hair would have looked nice had it been brushed. She seemed unaware that a slight smile and a soft look in her eye would instantly render her a pretty girl. This troubled girl had just remarked that she saw no reason for being alive. "What difference does it make?" she had asked, as she described a life that had been marred by continuous arguments with her mother.

What difference does it make? That question demands an answer from all teenagers as they look down the long road of life ahead of them. For many, the road looks like smooth sailing. For others, life resembles miles and miles of potholes. It certainly seemed that way to this young person. She certainly had good reason for her negative outlook. Her past had been quite rude to her, offering her little hope for a more congenial future.

In spite of her young age, Sharon seriously questioned the value of her short life. The question continued to plague her, *"What difference does it make?"* She had reached the frightening conclusion that she, and others, would be better off dead. She didn't really know how to end her life, but she did what she could by swallowing fifty aspirin with a glass of milk. A friend had convinced her this combination would do the trick, but it only nauseated her.

She decided if she could not kill herself, she would do the next best thing. She collected a few favored items and left home, intending never to return. She stayed away two days and one night, but gave in to hunger and discomfort and finally called her worried mother to come and pick her up.

Sometimes It Hurts to Feel

Many teenagers feel anger so strongly that it clouds their feelings. All the teen can say is, "I hurt, but I don't know where it comes from." The ever-present anger makes little sense to the young person as she desperately grasps to understand herself. Sharon made statements that indicated pain, but could not comprehend her hurt. She made the following comments at various times:

- *I'm lonely. Nobody knows who I am.*
- *If I started screaming, it would take hours to get all my feelings out.*
- *Everybody tells me to keep my chin up. But if I put my chin up, someone will just pull it right back down.*
- *I don't even want to know what other people think about me. If I found out, I'd just feel hurt all over again.*
- *My mother always tells me life isn't supposed to be fair. Why isn't it? It seems pretty fair to everybody but me.*

Sharon's life experiences had taught her all the wrong lessons. Though entering what should have been the most exciting time of her life, she was persuaded that nothing good awaited her. She had become afraid to feel her emotions. She could not say what she felt. She was unsure about trusting others. To her, life hurt.

Life Can Cripple Emotional Growth

We sometimes think only adults can look at the past with hurt and resentment. We assume that the teenager's short walk through

38

life precludes an understanding of what life is really about. It is true that the adolescent's life experience is too limited to adequately judge its value. Yet many teens jump to hasty conclusions about life based on their limited experiences.

Because of her youth, Sharon could not accurately explain why life was no good. She simply defined life as nothing but disappointment and hard knocks. Her exasperated mother once asked her how such a young girl could so convincingly state that life was the pits. Desperate for understanding, Sharon blurted out, "Look what you've put me through and decide for yourself if it's been any good!"

Sharon's mother felt that life really was not as bad as her daughter seemed to think. Asked to give some details of Sharon's life, Nancy blushed, but consented. "I don't really like to talk about my family, because people might get the wrong idea. When you hear what we've been through, it sounds worse than it really was. You see, what Sharon doesn't like is the way her father and I used to get along when we were married. She is convinced that he was an alcoholic, but I don't really think so. Sure, he drank a lot, but he would sometimes go weeks without even one drink. Do you call that an alcoholic?" A noncommittal gesture encouraged her to proceed with her story.

"He and I didn't get along very well, even from the start. Sharon was born shortly after we were married. I think that had a lot to do with our marital problems. You see, he didn't want children. Sharon knew it and assumed he didn't love her. He loved her; he just wasn't the kind of man who did much with children. I think he still loves her, although Sharon will tell you he doesn't."

Trying to understand what Nancy was relating, I commented, "So you and your husband never got along, and Sharon was partly to blame for your problems. When did she start to show she was unhappy with her life?"

Nancy chuckled. "I can't think of a time that she wasn't mad about something. She's that kind of girl." Nervously, she frowned and continued. "Sharon's father and I divorced when Sharon was six years old. But you might as well say that we didn't really end it all until about two years ago. We kept getting back together and then breaking up again. I decided things weren't getting any better, so I finally bailed out of the relationship. We haven't heard much from him since then. He calls every now and then, but only to talk to Sharon. She gets mad at me every time she talks to her father. I tell her not to take it out on me, but she does anyway."

"What do you think Sharon is trying to say when she gets upset at you?"

"Probably that she's mad at me for taking away her father. I don't really know what the problem is."

The statement from Nancy, "I don't really know what the problem is," bothered Sharon. She had privately concluded that her mother never would understand. Sharon was convinced that she was trapped in a family that wore blinders and that frightened her. She was afraid to trust her own feelings. She was afraid to express her feelings. She was also afraid to ask others, especially those close to her, what they felt about her. She was crippled by her own fear and the anger it provoked.

Anger Can Make a Teen Stumble

A teen's emotions are intended to help, rather than to hinder, an adolescent. Through parental guidance, the teen can learn to:

- choose appropriate times to make angry feelings known
- experience the richness of all human emotions
- understand others' feelings as well as her own
- guard against feelings of personal defeat
- interact meaningfully with others in need
- accept and give emotional support
- feel relief from the tensions that make life unbearable

When, however, conflict hovers over the home, anger becomes a millstone around the teen's neck rather than a potential asset. In a healthy home atmosphere anger is in its proper place.

Sharon's story of her family history differed from her mother's version. Sharon told of how she had been hurt by her own angry feelings. "My mom and dad pretend that they didn't get along all that bad. Ha! All I ever remember is how they fought with each other. And most of the time it was about me! How do you think that makes me feel?"

Nancy defended herself saying, "Sharon, you're looking at it all wrong! I'll admit your father and I argued a lot. But, if you want to know what a really argumentative family is like, you should have been in *my* home when I was a girl. If you could have seen the way your grandparents fought, you'd be thankful things weren't any worse than they were in our home. I can only tell you things were *really* bad for me."

Sharon rolled her eyes as she listened to her mother. She had heard those words too many times before. "Let me guess, Sharon," I interjected. "You and your mother have already been through this conversation." In unison Sharon and Mother nodded their heads. "And I'll bet you don't agree on whose past is worst, yours or hers." Again, there was simultaneous agreement between mother and daughter.

Anger had become a stumbling block for Sharon's family. Its intensity had gripped generations of victims. Sharon and Nancy were asked momentarily to step away from their own emotions and inspect their family history as an outsider might observe it. Both struggled with this exercise, but tried to be objective.

After a few minutes, Nancy insightfully said, "I guess I look at Sharon's life the way I looked at my own family life, even though we're talking about two different families. Maybe that gets in my way when I try to understand Sharon."

Sharon was encouraged to respond to her mother. A calmer

young person shared her thoughts, "Mom, I've always felt that if I told you what I really think, you're just going to tell me I shouldn't feel that way. How can I tell myself not to feel the way I feel?"

Sharon and her mother had discovered a vicious cycle of angry defeat in their family. They had both been victimized by years of unchecked emotions. Nancy was a victim to the anger of her family of origin. Sharon, in turn, had also fallen prey to ineffective anger.

Victims Tend to Find Blame

A peculiar thing happens to those of us who have come out of a long line of emotional mismanagement. We tend to look for someone to bear the blame for our troubles. Sharon did it in a number of ways. She:

- complained that her parents did not show her the affection she wanted and needed
- refused to accept responsibility for her mistakes, claiming it was her parents' fault
- resisted "giving in" to her parents for fear of losing control of her own emotions
- claimed that her impulsive outbursts were no worse than her parents'
- held on to her "right" to feel and act the way she did

While Sharon's thoughts and actions may be hard to swallow, they almost make sense in light of her mother's behavior to sidestep responsibility for her adult behavior in ways listed below. Nancy:

- turned a blind eye to the effects of her home environment on Sharon
- excused her behavior by claiming that she acted better toward her daughter than her parents had acted toward her
- rationalized that she had come out of her childhood relatively sound, and assumed Sharon would do the same

- reasoned that she had tried giving her daughter a chance at a normal family life by attempting to make things work with Sharon's father
- criticized Sharon for being so negative and failing to appreciate the good things life had offered her

As we examine family histories, we often find that a pattern of hurt is passed from one generation to another. Young adults tend to interpret life based on the climate in which they were raised. After all, the world of our childhood is the only world we have ever known. One of the gratifying developments of adulthood is the ability to understand the past in a way that eluded us in our youth.

Each parent has the God-given capacity to fill in the missing pieces of our past by reshaping our interpretation of life. Yet, so many of us choose to passively believe that life probably will not change much as we grow. A child can then fall victim to the same emotional trap which snared her parents. From generation to generation, one of the most common traps is anger!

Teenagers caught in a web of cyclical anger, like Sharon, feel confused and embittered. Emotions tend to be felt in extremes. The teen will trek through life with limp emptiness, or with vengeance. There is little middle ground. An angry victim may think some of the thoughts below.

- *I don't know when I'm supposed to be angry and when I'm supposed to be calm, so I'll just choose to be angry.*
- *I'm so mixed up, I don't know what I think anymore.*
- *I know it's not nice to feel angry. I must not be a nice person.*
- *If I try to hold my anger in, I can't! If I try to let it out, I'm told I can't.*
- *People tell me to be normal when I express my anger. What's that?*
- *People probably hate me the way I hate myself for being angry all the time.*

Teens who are caught in a cycle of family anger do not know what to feel or how to feel. They simply do what they can to make sense of their muddled emotions. A parent's emotional expression can confirm or deny the value of the teen's emotional choices. Adolescents learn plenty about anger, good or bad, from adult family members.

Help Your Teen Break the Victim's Cycle

A guiding truth of family life states that adults are in a position to offer positive leadership because of their advanced experience. Experience being the great teacher it is, parenthood gives adults the chance to pass wisdom to their developing children—a noble thought. Yet life slaps us with the reality that adults are full of holes and weaknesses. We all enter adulthood with our unique set of worries and faults. It is normal for parents to look for ways to protect their children against life's frailties. For example, we may:

- deny the reality of our past's most harmful experiences
- rationalize our behavior, thus choosing to ignore the harm we are passing along to our children
- "pass the buck" to someone else as a way of avoiding responsibility
- hold too firmly to our convictions with the hope of forcing safety on our child's world
- bite off more than we can swallow by trying to be all things to all people
- ignore the hurts of the past with the hope that they will disappear

The parent must engage the cycle of change in order for a teenager to understand and manage anger. The parent, as family leader, must first be released from anger's effect before it will loosen its grip on the other family members. We can all quickly agree that hostile parents do untold damage to the teens who imitate them. The parent who shows no anger at all also harms the teen. A parent at either extreme of angry expression offers an incomplete picture of healthy emotional development.

I view parents as instruments of God who are used to guide and direct impressionable youth toward eventual satisfaction. The more a parent is completely "herself," the more likely she is to be effective as she guides the growth process of the young person. A healthy adult once described her father as follows: "I never really worried that my dad was being unreal around me. I knew that his emotions were real. If he was happy with himself, he took the chance to pass along his good feelings to the rest of us. When he was angry, like all of us are from time to time, he was aware of his emotions. He made a point to use his anger appropriately, but he didn't let it tear down the respect I had for him."

Anger in a family need not be ignored. In fact, it cannot be ignored. A major task of adolescence is to uncover the value of all emotions so they can be used as they were intended. Young people know when they are living with an adult who is the "real thing." Parental openness and honesty with anger helps release a teen from the harmful clutches of a potentially victimizing emotion.

Section Two

THE MANY MASKS
OF TEENAGE ANGER

◆

CHAPTER SIX

The Match That Lights the Fire

WHEN THE TEEN EXPLODES WITH ANGER

I t is interesting to ask teenagers questions about themselves. We think we know their thoughts, but when we dare to roam through their world, surprises often await us. I conducted an informal survey of teenagers who passed through my office to learn how they use anger destructively. These teens were posed two simple questions. The first was "What do you do that really upsets your parents?" Here are some of the reactions I received:

- I keep my room a mess on purpose
- I drag up their past mistakes
- I quit trying
- I look at them with a blank stare
- I use bad language
- I fail on purpose
- I hit my sibling

- I scream as loud as I can
- I interrupt them
- I make threats
- I get in the last word
- I do what I want to do
- I turn the stereo up loud
- I break things
- I hit my parent
- I won't go out with them

The second question was "What do your parents do when you have made them angry?" The teens answered:

- they make threats
- they give in
- they demand an answer

- they cry
- they yell and scream
- they give a lecture

- they drag up my past
- they tease me
- they say I'm a failure
- they fight with each other
- they force decisions on me

- they take everything away
- they have tantrums
- they hit (or spank) me
- they clam up
- they curse

Sometimes it hurts to hear what teens say about anger. It seems that they learn many tricks of their trade from us! Ouch! To make matters worse, I might add that many of these teens laughed or smiled as they gave away their thoughts. It was as if they were adding this nonverbal statement: *Here's how we operate. Just see if you can do anything to stop us!* It seems that adolescents have figured out how to use their angry expressions to get what they want. Too often it seems that they want revenge.

Teens Can Use Their Emotions to Hurt Others

From an early age children carefully observe their families. They notice what characterizes each family member. As if equipped with radar, they quickly learn how to "press buttons" to cause the reaction they desire. This learning process is not all bad. Through observation, children learn what makes their parents happy. If affirmed, children will likely repeat those behaviors that drew a favorable reaction from someone they love. Their learning is slanted negatively, though, when they learn to use anger as a means toward an end. Anger can become an aggressive tool the young person uses to take charge of the home atmosphere.

CASE STUDY: *Jamie Digs in Her Heels*

Jamie was having another bad day. Unfortunately, most of her days were of the same flavor. Her mother and father knew from daybreak that trouble lay ahead of them. The simple request to get out of bed for breakfast was rudely greeted with a growl. "Go away! I don't want any breakfast. How many times do I have to tell you?

If I want something to eat, I'll get it myself! I'm getting up. Leave me alone, will ya?" Her parents were amazed that she could put such force into her words and then plop down and go right back to sleep.

After the struggle to get her up and ready for school, Jamie aimlessly made her way through the day. She only did what she had to do at school, breezed through a few minutes of homework, and headed out the door yelling, "I'll be back later."

Her mother ran to the back door to remind Jamie, "You may have forgotten, but tonight's the night we asked you to stay here with us. Grandmother is coming over for dinner, and we told her you and your sister would both be here."

Unwilling to be told she could not go out and do as she pleased, Jamie screamed, "Mom, why do I always have to do what you want me to do? Why can't I do what I want for a change? What difference does it make if I'm not here when Grandmother comes over? Why can't you be satisfied if just Glenda is here and not me? She can talk to Grandmother for me. I'm going out!"

Now angry at Jamie's open defiance, the mother took the challenge as though her daughter had thrown down the gauntlet to duel. "Well, you can just forget it, young lady. Even if I had decided to change my mind to let you go, there's no way I'm giving in to that attitude! You're not going anywhere tonight! You have to stay home, because it would be impolite for us to invite Grandmother over to visit if no one is going to be home for the evening."

Remaining on the offensive, Jamie continued the assault on her mother. "All you care about is that we look like one big happy family! Why should I have to stay here tonight when you know I don't want to be here? I hate it when you make me stay here just because Grandmother is coming over! I can see her anytime. It's not like she lives a thousand miles away and we never get to see her."

Appealing to her daughter's sense of reason, Mom retorted, "Jamie, you know how much it means for your grandmother to see you and Glenda. And you always end up having a good time when she's here."

"Oh right! It's loads of fun to talk with Grandmother about what she's been doing all day. She's probably going to tell me all about what's been happening on her favorite TV shows. Big deal! Besides, why can't I just go over to Grandmother's house sometime this weekend and visit her then? I don't have to be around here tonight."

Like a fifteen round boxing match, the argument drudged on, with both mother and daughter using their best combination of punches. Their blows to each other took the form of sharp words, accusations, predictions, pleas, sarcasm, threats, and disrespect. The fight ended in a draw as both lost a match neither wanted to enter to begin with. Jamie spent the evening at home while her mother wound up with another headache.

Adolescence is commonly a time of storm and stress. Although it may help to know that many parents face the same struggles that go on in your home, that fact doesn't make these struggles any easier to handle. More than one parent has speculated that life would be easier if teenagers would simply recognize that cooperation is more appealing than constant fighting.

I believe that while trials and testing limits are a necessary part of adolescence, they need not get out of hand. The parent's reaction to teen anger can encourage it to either escalate or subside. The teen feels an urge to be independent in making decisions. To show that she is liberated from her need for adult authority, the teen will sometimes use extreme measures to show that she is on her own. Teens frequently complain of having to give in to adult authority. They quickly grow weary of playing second fiddle to adults, especially parents.

Something happens in the teenager's natural development that contributes to this resentment. During early adolescence, the young person develops the ability to think like an adult. By the end of the high school years, she will have matched an adult's thinking capacity. The teen is equally capable of coming to independent conclusions about a given situation as her parent.

However, one major factor separates teens from adults in their ability to think wisely: life experience. Through experience, adults have learned to judge the value of their thoughts and ideas. They can weigh their conclusions against their own past trials. Adults can see more objectively because life has taught them the error of plowing ahead with a plan that has no assurances attached.

Teens lack the experience that makes them equal to adults in wisdom and judgment. Though able to think much like adults, they come to different conclusions simply because they have not lived long enough. This single factor contributes heavily to a teenager's rebellion. A parent's controlled reaction to the young person's natural lack of judgment can diminish the intensity of teen anger.

Why Do Teenagers Ask Why?

When told she needed to stay in for the evening, Jamie's immediate reaction was to bombard her mother with a series of questions begining with the word "why." Do you really think Jamie wanted to know the reasons she had to stay home? Probably not. Most likely the word "why" held a different value to this teenager. Before she posed questions to her mother, she already had a good idea what the answers would be. By asking why, Jamie was simultaneously accomplishing several things. She was:

- shifting the attention from herself to her mother
- challenging the reasoning behind her mother's argument
- showing her immediate disapproval of her mother's rule
- inviting her mother to enter a war of words
- stating her wish to be allowed to make her own choices

Notice the reaction Jamie received when she blasted her mother with why questions: She successfully started a battle for control.

Jamie had one objective as she exploded in anger—to win the war she had just started with her mom.

There are two ways a teenager can win a battle in which anger is the primary assault weapon. First, she could push her mother into total surrender. Jamie would feel triumphant if she coerced her mother into letting her go out and do her own thing. We could call that ploy Plan A. But just as a field general has a backup plan, so does the teenager have another design in case Plan A fails.

Wanting to gain some semblance of victory, Jamie's second plan would be to take control of her mother's emotions. Jamie would accept the consolation prize of dictating the mood of the home. In this case, her intent would be to cause others to share her own foul mood. Or, Jamie could simply leave the house to do as she pleased, totally disregarding her mother's request. She would have gloated in victory as her steamed mother helplessly watched her drive away. Even the certainty of later punishment would override her pleasure of shoving her mother into an angry stew.

Teenagers recognize the parent's tendency to respond to "why" questions with "because" answers. We may not actually use this word as we speak, but it is implied. We send messages that state:

- because it's the rule
- because I said so
- because I know what's best for you
- because I don't think you make wise choices
- because I'm in charge around here
- because you got your way the last time
- because you need a dose of humility

Teenagers ask why questions in order to debate the value of the parent's decision. When Jamie was told she had to stay home because it was impolite to ask a guest over without giving her a warm welcome, she knew she had a good opportunity to argue. She could correctly maintain that her mother's rule was neither right nor wrong. It simply depended on the situation at hand. She could argue that since their evening guest was only her grandmother, rules of etiquette could be relaxed. Or she could promise to drop by her grandmother's house at a later date to say "hello." There were an endless number of points she could make to win the control battle with her mother.

Choose Not to Debate

It is natural and normal for parents to want a teenager to accept their leadership. That desire is what motivates parents to argue with an angry teen. The hope is to convince the young person to let go of her stubborn insistence to see things her way and accept a more experienced judgment.

In parenthood, it is important to balance the choices we make with the reality of adolescent development. If adolescence is a time when teenagers willingly match thoughts and ideas with adults, the wise adult will choose not to engage in arguments with that opinionated young person.

Here are some statements adolescents make when asked about their debates with parents:

- *My parents always think their way is better than mine. I hate that!*
- *I don't like to be forced to do anything. I like to make my own decisions.*
- *I'd rather learn from my own mistakes. But I don't want anyone to say, "I told you so."*
- *Sometimes I like being the rebel of the family.*
- *If I let my parents win an argument, they'll gloat.*
- *My parents think they know what's best for me. How can they know? It's been so long since they were my age.*
- *When my parents and I argue, there's no way I'm giving in—even if it means punishment.*

For the teenager to learn to make wise choices, it is sometimes necessary that she plod through normal adolescent rebellion. The parent should concede that the teenager will disagree. It is inevitable. When the parent responds to teenage anger with adult anger, the only possible result is an angry family. But answering teenage anger with adult control increases the likelihood of eventual family unity.

Parents should be quick to recognize the beginnings of teen anger. Most of the time, those signs can hardly be ignored. A red face, a scowl, a bitter tone of voice, a tense pose all point to a pending explosion.

When Jamie was told she could not go out for the evening, she showed all the telltale signs of a pending burst of anger. Her mother's efforts to reason with Jamie failed. We must assume that only Jamie can decide just how angry she will be. There is no need to provoke that anger to greater heights by trying to push it aside with logic.

When Jamie initially stressed her displeasure at her mother's reminder that her grandmother was coming over for dinner, her mother could have retreated from that anger without giving in to Jamie's desire to take charge. A simple statement from the mother could have acknowledged Jamie's discontent. "I know that's not what you wanted to hear" would have told Jamie that her feelings were not being denied.

It is almost certain that Jamie would present a challenge to her mother, despite the parent's understanding response. Her mother's understanding way would not erase the teen's desire to control her immediate destiny. The bombardment of "why" questions is still likely. At that point, it is important that the parent maintain her leadership. Realizing that the word "why" is an invitation to fight, the parent should control her own anger to avoid handing the controls of the home to the inexperienced teen.

"I can't make you like the situation" is all that needs to be said. After that, physically withdraw from the teen. To stand and wait for a response suggests a willingness to debate. The parent who withdraws is making the statement, "I give you the right to your anger. To try to help you keep your anger from getting out of hand, I will refuse to get angry at you. I know that would only make it more difficult for you to learn from your experience."

And what if Jamie had decided to leave the house anyway, ignoring her mother's authority? The mother would not have been without options. Once Jamie returned home, the mother could have expressed her displeasure: "Jamie, I was very upset when you left the house knowing that I wanted you to be home while Grandmother was here." Almost certainly, Jamie would have offered an excuse for her defiance: "For your information, Mother, I had already promised Rachael that I would take her to the mall to shop for her father's birthday. What do you want me to do, let my friend down? No way!"

Seeing Jamie's defiant excuse as yet another invitation to fight, Mother should wisely decline the invitation by saying, "I think we could have worked things out, but there's no use arguing over what's already happened."

The next time Jamie wanted a favor or privilege from Mother, her request should be calmly denied since Jamie had not recently shown the cooperation deserving of special treatment. Again, emotional composure, not vindication, should characterize the adult's reaction. Keeping words to a minimum keeps the parent, not the teenager, in the leadership position.

A parent who fails to control her own anger in the presence of the teen's anger fails to teach wisdom. Forcing "the facts" on a young person keeps the teen from appreciating those truths. Allowing the teen to conclude for herself how she will handle the dilemmas of family life encourages her to respect the facts of life. The parent's responsibility is to set guidelines within which the teen may learn how to get along in a world that says no to uncontrolled anger.

CHAPTER SEVEN

◆

I'm Too Nice to Be Angry

TEEN ANGER CAN BE SUBTLE

Davd's mother was concerned about her son. "He's such a sweet boy, I don't want to see him hurt so badly." Pain was all over her face, obviously grieved by her son's discomfort.

"In what ways is David hurting?"

"I don't really know. He won't tell me. I've repeatedly asked him to share with me what he feels. He promises me, though, that nothing is wrong."

"But you don't believe him. There's probably more to David's feelings than he's willing to tell."

"That's what it seems to me. If he weren't upset, I don't think he'd act the way he does, do you?"

Mrs. Bell sought help for David because of a slow decline in his behavior. He was not, and never had been, a "bad" child. Oh sure, he broke rules from time to time, but nothing out of the ordinary. Over the previous six months, he had dropped most of his regular activities. He no longer drove the remote control car he previously loved to take to a local race track. He was disinterested in social activities, frequently declining offers from friends to get together on weekends. His school performance dropped, although he still managed to make acceptable grades.

What bothered David's mother most among his "new" behaviors was his clingy attachment to her. She explained, "He was like that as a small child, but he outgrew his shyness the way most children do. It seems that he's going backward instead of forward in his maturity. I feel that I have a little boy on my hands again. He won't let me do anything unless he checks on me to make sure I'm alright."

"Have you wondered what it is that has caused David to act as he has? What thoughts have run through your mind?" I asked.

Mrs. Bell stared out the window as if she hoped to find an answer as she spoke. "At first I thought maybe he was reacting to my divorce from his father, but I don't think that's the problem. His dad and I have been divorced for seven years. My other son doesn't think David is bothered by that anymore. I took on a new job three years ago that requires me to be gone a lot at night, but I don't see how that could be the problem. I check up on him regularly while I'm at work, and he assures me he doesn't resent my schedule. I don't know what the problem is with him."

Anger Can Go Underground

We tend to look at anger as a highly visible emotion. We assume that the angry teen will show the world his emotions as he erupts into a colorful tantrum. However, all anger is not displayed so boldly. Anger often hides beneath a teen's other behaviors. The masked anger of a teenager can have a deadly impact on a family, doing as much damage as explosive anger.

Raucous, rebellious teenagers do not have a lock on anger. Even the most respectful adolescent can play games with this emotion. Unlike his rebellious counterpart, the more sensitive teenager deceives himself with his emotional silence as much as he tries to fool others. It is as though this teen has vowed: *I refuse to be an angry person, but if I do become angry, I refuse to let anyone know my feelings.*

David was a difficult child to get close to though he was certainly easy to like. His manners were straight from an Emily Post manual. He could hold a pleasant conversation with adults. In my office, he spoke clearly of his desire to do what he could to make his family a more cohesive unit once again. Yet, he held a shield in front of him that was difficult to penetrate.

When asked about his parents' divorce and its impact on him, David shrugged his shoulders. "Oh, it really doesn't bother me. I think about it now and then and wish they hadn't done it, but I guess there's no use wishing for something that you know you can't change. I made up my mind a long time ago not to worry about it."

There was a strong hint of deception in his message. He did not seem so intent on deceiving me as much as he wanted to convince himself that he didn't feel hurt. He wasn't doing such a good job.

David consented to keep a journal of his thoughts to share with me each time he visited my office. We agreed that only I would read them—no one else. One of his journal entries read: *We talked about my parents' divorce last time. The more I think about it, the madder I get. Parents who get a divorce are only thinking about themselves. They don't even think about the hurt their kids go through. I ought to know. I'm one of those kids.*

David's written words confirmed my suspicions that his anger was more intense than he would admit. For seven years this young man had battled his feelings about a family trauma. His fear of losing the family closeness he desired was unfortunately being realized. But David gave a curious response when I asked him to comment on his journal entry.

"David, this is an interesting note you've written about your parents' divorce. Tell me more about what you were thinking."

David's face was blank. He held out his hand for the journal. Reading the entry he had penned only days earlier, he seemed genuinely surprised that he had actually written those words. The look on his face said, *Yep, that's my handwriting, alright, but I certainly don't recognize those words.*

After a moment of study, he could only say, "Huh. I guess I must have been thinking about what you said the last time we talked." He could go no further in the conversation.

I find that young people who go underground with their anger honestly do not know that this emotion exists—at least not as intensely as others see it. This adolescent often believes:

- *If I can convince others that I am not angry, then I will have also successfully convinced myself.*
- *Others will not think I am a nice guy if I openly show my anger. I had better sweep it under the rug.*
- *By remaining cool and calm on the outside, I'll be able to keep the relationships I have.*
- *If I let my angry feelings show, I'm afraid no one can possibly understand the way I feel.*
- *If I ignore the emotional churning inside, surely it will go away soon.*

Teenagers as sensitive as David are simultaneously the most pleasurable and the most difficult to be around. Their manners, eagerness to please, and outward concern for others is attractive. But their tendency to hide their emotions, deny feelings, and ignore signs of emotional danger keep relationships on a surface level. His fear can detach him from others even though he badly wants close relationships.

Anger May Isolate a Teenager

It's funny how our emotions work. No matter how hard we try, we simply cannot ignore them. When a teenager attempts to push aside strong feelings, they insist on popping up when they are most unwelcome. It is as if the teen is doomed to defeat in a fight against an unwanted emotion. Unless the teenager accepts his emotions as a force to be reckoned with, they will continually plague him. Such was the case with David. He struggled to hide his emotions behind a smiling face, but had limited success. To be sure, he was pretty successful in convincing his friends of his self-satisfaction. But his mother knew otherwise. Hard as it was for him to admit, David knew differently too.

David had assumed that by minding his own business and ignoring the events around him, he could stay ahead of the despair his anger pressed on him. He honestly believed that by disengaging from family problems, he could avoid being hurt. He was disgusted when his hopes were dashed during his teen years.

I commented to him once, "You know, David, people are saying things about you that I'm sure make you feel uncomfortable. They point to your low grades in school and claim that you're not as motivated as you used to be. Your mom wonders why you don't do things you used to love doing. People are noticing that you turn down chances to be with your friends. I think others worry that you're not yourself anymore. What do you think?"

David could only shake his head. He tried to make some words come out of his mouth, but they got stuck somewhere between his heart and his throat. Helplessly, he managed only a weak shrug of his shoulders.

"Let me try to help. You probably know that your mother and others are right to be concerned for you. Things have been going downhill for the last few months, haven't they?" David gave a slight nod. "You know, David, you're such a nice guy, it's hard for you to say anything that may hurt someone else's feelings. For example, you'd probably like to say some things to your parents that you've just never said before."

A peculiar look came over his face. His eyes shot out the message, *Don't say what I'm thinking. That's taboo!* At the same time, his heart screamed, *Go ahead and say what I'm thinking. The weight on me is so heavy I can hardly stand it!*

"Like what?" came his controlled response.

"Let's make a list and see what you'd like to say to your family."

Looking for reassurance David quickly blurted out, "We don't have to show my mom, do we?" I persuaded him that the list of thoughts would be between him and me. He slowly bobbed his head up and down. The thoughts we generated included:

- *I want to be liked—no, loved—by others.*
- *If I tell you how I really feel, you will reject me.*
- *I want my feelings to be considered when family decisions are made.*
- *I don't want to be hurt.*
- *When you ask me how you should handle your problems, I feel pressured. I want you to be the leader of our family.*
- *I just want life to go on without any problems.*
- *I hate to feel upset. Please don't do anything that makes me feel that way.*
- *Even though I say I don't care, I really do.*
- *I miss you when I'm not around you. I'm afraid you'll find a way to live without me.*

As with David, anger can steal intimate relationships from any teenager. Some young people are naturally more sensitive than others. Their feelings are hurt more quickly than most. They read more into a given situation than was intended. Emotions are felt strongly, but bottled inside. Time takes its toll on this young person. Perhaps he can temporarily fend off the emotional urge to express his anger. But anger will always find a way out. In David's case, it was through a loss of motivation.

A teenager with a "nice guy" image will find a cost attached to maintaining this status. It is a high cost, too—the loss of relationships and the lack of love. For the teenager who is too kind to openly admit to anger, it becomes a barrier in relationships. But because anger *always* prevails in internal power struggles, choking this emotion backfires on the teen. His greatest fear—loss of closeness with others—is realized because he denies the anger that drives people away.

Parents May Help Anger Stay Hidden

Mrs. Bell did not intend to encourage David to push his emotions underground. She sensed that her son was emotionally sensitive and did not want to do anything that might damage him. She did all she could to make life easier for him. For example, she:

- did not talk about topics she knew bothered David
- refrained from pressuring David to perform at too high a level
- gave in to David's request to be left alone, assuming he knew what he needed from her
- made exceptions for David, hoping that he would appreciate her even more
- blamed herself for David's apparent unhappiness

A parent may have the best intentions for a child, only to later realize that her well-intended reactions provided fertilizer for a growing anger. When anger is ignored, it spreads like a fungus in the young person. A highly sensitive teen has a way of becoming dependent on a parent. By hiding in the comfort of a parent's protection, the youth can delay, sometimes for years, an inevitable confrontation with anger. Until that showdown comes, though, the teen hopes beyond hope that anger will simply give up and go away. It won't.

Mrs. Bell and I talked about how David's silent anger impacted the family communication system. She explained, "I've just learned through the years not to say anything that will upset David. I know he takes things the wrong way, so I figure it's better to just leave well enough alone."

Trying to help her understand how David's silent anger affected the family, I asked: "But doesn't this keep you and your children from having the kind of open communication you would like?"

Mrs. Bell sighed. "I'm sure it does. I can talk with my other son about certain things I wouldn't dare mention to David. He gets upset over the least little problem. We've just learned to sidestep sensitive topics in our home. That's probably not right, but life sure is easier that way."

Of course, many of the decisions we adults make directly affect our family life. We may influence our children by consciously choosing to confront potential family problems. Or, we may guide our children through the decisions we *don't* make. By deciding not to broach sensitive subjects with David, Mrs. Bell essentially gave him the nod to decide how he would deal with anger. He chose to ignore it!

David struggled to find the right words anytime the subject of communication came up in family discussions. He usually attempted to change the subject to a more pleasant topic. If his attempt was unsuccessful, he would clam up. Not only was his silence a protest, it also showed his inability to handle anger.

Teens Need Help Identifying Their Emotions

Good parents want to communicate well with their children. It is normal to want a teenager to be happy and content. We may assume, though, that sidestepping difficult emotions will help a young person as he struggles with himself. A teen may feel temporary relief at not having to face touchy subjects, but the long-term effect of withheld emotions can be destructive. Consider some of the important tasks of adolescence. The teen must learn to:

- make choices independently
- become self-sufficient in caring for personal needs
- create a support network among his peer group
- assert himself appropriately toward adults
- make sense of who he is emotionally, socially, and spiritually
- understand what others are trying to communicate to him

To meet those needs favorably, the teen must first learn to recognize his own emotions. Once recognized, he must know how to express those emotions in a useful way. The parent of a teen who runs from anger faces a tough choice: to allow the youth to ignore his emotions or to help him confront them. While neither choice may be particularly pleasant, the obvious need of the teen is to confront his own dreaded anger.

I know what you're thinking. If the parent is to help the reserved teen recognize his anger, how can this task be accomplished without blowing the roof off the family's home? It can be done.

Mrs. Bell told of a time that she tried to help David understand his anger. "He came home with a test paper on which he had made a 72. That's a lot lower than he was used to making. I couldn't believe how he was just accepting grades like that. He had always taken such pride in his school work. I asked him what he thought about his grade. Do you know what he did? He just shrugged his shoulders and mumbled. He didn't care!"

Trying to imagine the scene, I asked Mrs. Bell, "How do you think David would have reacted if you had said, 'Sometimes you reach the point that it's hard to care about school, don't you?'"

A quizzical look appeared on her face. "You mean I should have agreed with him that it didn't matter what grade he made?"

"No, I'm wondering what he would have done if you had simply said aloud what you already knew he was thinking."

"Hmm. I never thought of that. What do you think?"

"Maybe he would have felt relieved that he wasn't all alone with his disgust with himself. Just maybe he would have told you a little more of what was churning through his head at the time."

An archaeologist friend of mine explains how he learns of history by digging through one layer at a time. Our emotions are like that. Through the years, we pile one experience on top of another until a mountain of feelings lays uncovered within us. To get to the bottom of that emotional pile we must dig down through the layers of rubble. As the teen sorts out his emotions, life's challenges become clearer.

A teenager needs help peeling back feelings to get at the root of emotions like anger. The parent can help him uncover them with timely statements. As a teenager learns to label his emotions, he understands himself more completely. With an understanding of his emotions comes the capacity to make wiser choices. Those wise choices, in turn, lead to a greater degree of responsibility in the young person. A positive cycle of thinking replaces destructive anger.

The parent can help the teen who turns emotions inward by:

- temporarily putting herself in the child's shoes in order to think as the teen thinks
- identifying the thoughts and emotions the teen must be experiencing at the moment
- stating in words the teen can understand the thoughts it appears he is thinking
- allowing the teen to react to the statement that has been made to him
- listening as the teen makes further comments about what he thinks or feels
- allowing the teen to come to conclusions about what he will do with his emotions

Let's reconstruct Mrs. Bell's conversation with David about his poor test grade. She has just said to her son, "Sometimes you reach the point that it's hard to care about your school work, don't you?"

David simply mumbles, "Yeah. I hate school."

Sensing his defeat, Mom replies, "School was a lot more fun when your grades were good. It's a drag when you have to struggle to pass."

Looking up, David says with a little more expression, "I wish it weren't so hard."

"You could get excited about your school work if you knew you were going to glide right through without any problems."

Digging deeper into his thoughts, David says, "I sure wish that would happen. That'd be nice."

Knowing that David is aware of the cost of making good grades in school, his mom remarks, "That would take more effort, wouldn't it?"

Nodding, David states, "Um hmm. I haven't been doing that." Mom waits silently, recognizing that her son is thinking. She leaves him with the responsibility of deciding what to do with his situation.

When a parent helps a child peel away his thoughts and emotions, she puts him in a more likely position to constructively deal with his anger. In this scenario, if David had been left alone with the disappointment over his poor showing in school, he probably would have turned his anger inward. He would have assumed that he was an irresponsible person who simply couldn't live up to his potential. Or he might have blamed his teacher, or even his mother, for his failure.

By walking a teen though his emotions, anger gives way to action. Rather than simmering inside like a boiling pot, the teen's angry feelings are brought to the foreground. The young person is then more likely to try to rid himself of an unwanted emotion and is less likely to view anger as a stumbling block to relationships.

A sensitive teen can be gently taught to control his anger. And anger can become a helpful tool that motivates change, rather than a silent rope that chokes the enthusiasm from life.

◆

CHAPTER EIGHT

There's a Poison Inside

ANGER CAN BE DECEIVING

Teenagers know when they are honest and when they are not—even though it may not seem that way. Most teens state that they want to be completely honest with their parents about their feelings, but often they feel compelled to disguise their emotions because they are afraid that their honest expression will not be accepted. Here are some remarks teenagers make about the deceptive ways they show their emotions:

- *If I say what I really think, no one will take me seriously.*
- *They'll just tell me I'm not allowed to say that.*
- *I get criticized when I say what's deep down inside.*
- *My parents just want to make all my decisions for me.*
- *I get tired of listening to my parents' constant advice.*
- *If I let them know how I really feel, I'll get in trouble.*
- *I don't want them to worry about me. I can take care of myself.*
- *My parents always assume the worst about me.*

As a parent, I can look on both sides of parent-teen communication and understand the good intentions of the adult. No parent wants to see a child endure unnecessary hardship and heartache. When parents intervene in their teenager's affairs, it is almost always with the intent to push their child toward contentment. Yet, best intentions aside, teenagers are prone to push away unsolicited instruction and guidance from parents. It is as though they are unconvinced of their parents' good intentions.

The independent-minded adolescent will often go to destructive lengths to hide his emotions. His desire is to be grown-up, self-sufficient, and independent. Capable or not, young people long to make choices without adult interference. The teen who feels pressured by adults to make the "right" decisions in life will express his anger deceitfully. The anger will be quite obvious, but the underlying meaning will be vague.

CASE STUDY: *Charlie's Caught in a Lie*

Charlie called to his mother as he left the house, "I'll be at Lance's house if you need me." He had no intention of even seeing Lance that evening, but felt obligated to leave his mother word of his whereabouts. Charlie drove directly to the house of his new girlfriend, Marie, hoping she could ride around with him in his car. He had no special plans. He simply wanted to spend time with her.

Marie's parents knew Charlie and approved of him. He was nice enough and was pretty clean-cut. He seemed like a normal kid. They told their daughter she could go out for awhile, but cautioned her to be in at a given time. After cruising the streets and talking aimlessly, Charlie and Marie pulled into the parking lot of a local teen hangout, hoping to meet some of their friends. Unknown to Charlie, his sister, Ann, was inside the restaurant eating pizza with a group of her friends. Seeing her brother with a new girlfriend excited her. She knew that news of the twosome would provide fresh gossip for her circle of friends.

Arriving home before Charlie, Ann immediately told her parents what she had seen. "Guess what? I was at Gino's eating pizza when Charlie came driving up with Marie Percell. My friends and I were watching them from inside the restaurant. You can tell Charlie really likes her by the way he was acting. He's a different person when girls are around. He tries to impress them with how cool he is."

Mom and Dad were interested in Ann's story, but not because of the intrigue of a budding romance. They asked Ann a few questions without betraying their intentions of confronting Charlie later that night.

When Charlie strolled into the house later in the evening, Mom and Dad were still awake. Showing apparent interest in his son's evening, Dad asked, "So, what did you and Lance do this evening?"

Charlie nonchalantly replied, "Oh, we just went down to the park and watched the Little League playoffs. Some of those games are pretty interesting." Charlie felt no guilt over his story since he and Marie had actually driven by the ballpark.

Dad continued his questioning. "Did you see anyone you know?"

"Nah. Just the usual guys. Nobody special."

Mother was poised to explode as she heard her son tell what she knew was a naked lie. Interrupting the trivial conversation between father and son, she blurted out, "Charlie, why are you telling us that story? We already know where you were tonight! Ann told us she saw you in the parking lot at Gino's with that Percell girl. Why do you have to tell us a lie? We don't mind if you see her. From what I know of her, she's a decent girl. You didn't have to tell us you were going to Lance's house when you knew you weren't. Why do you lie to us?"

Charlie was quiet outwardly, but a volcano was boiling within. He thought, *Just wait until I get a minute with Ann. I'll get even with her. And just what difference does it make if my parents know what I'm doing? It's none of their business anyway. I hate it that I'm seventeen years old and still have to tell them where I'm going and who I'm going to be with. I can do what I want to do. I don't have to explain myself to anyone! Besides, I haven't done anything wrong.*

"Answer your mother, Charlie. I think you owe us an explanation. You've been dishonest, and we want to know why." Charlie's dad wore a stern face.

Charlie refused to cooperate. "What difference does it make? I'm home, aren't I? I didn't do anything wrong! Tell your cute little daughter to mind her own business. I can't stand her!" He then turned to walk out of the room.

"Wait a minute, Charlie!" Dad called after him. "We're not through talking yet."

Charlie never broke stride as he went to his bedroom muttering to himself, "You may not be through talking, but I am." As he passed his sister's room he verbally jabbed her, "Just shut up the next time you feel like talking about me!"

The Desire for Independence Can Spur Anger

Try to recall your first job as an adult. You were fresh out of school and ready to join the work force. Regardless of your prior training, an uncertain feeling rumbled through your stomach. You watched how others worked to ensure you were doing the right thing. You even asked questions as a safeguard against mistakes. It was important that others recognized your work efforts. You hoped someone would tell you how well you were doing. It was probably unpleasant when a supervisor or coworker reprimanded you, even if you needed a jolt.

Like an adult in a new occupation, adolescents are in training to be adults. They have left childhood and eagerly face a grown-up world. They may have some of the ability required to get along with others, but their skills certainly are far from fine-tuned. They have the same need for direction in life that an employee has in learning a new job. Adolescents enjoy receiving compliments on a job well-done. They dislike any hint of disapproval from others, even if they deserve it. They differ from a newly hired employee, though, in that they are often more brazen in voicing their dislike of the negative feedback they might receive. After all, teens know they cannot be "fired" for doing a poor job as an adolescent. The job is theirs for several years.

Young people want to act like adults, but do not want to be told how to live life. In a teen's mind, to be told of an error is tantamount to being called a failure. Nobody wants to be called a failure at anything. Because of that dual desire to be treated like an adult and with limited interference, the teen is ripe for the very thing he hopes to dodge—failure.

Charlie made an error in judgment as he left the house to visit his new girlfriend. He should have thought before he told a lie, reminding himself that he could sidestep potential arguments by being truthful. He would have avoided the confrontation that faced him later in the evening. He wanted to be treated like an adult. ("I want to do what I want to do. I don't have to explain myself to anyone!") He wanted to feel that he could make choices without interference from family members.

Most teenagers would be surprised to discover that their parents have the very same goals for them as they have for themselves! If asked, Charlie's parents would have applauded their son's desire to make independent decisions. After all, that is a desire all parents have—to see their children live independently while simultaneously making wise choices. In the same way that teenagers want to assume responsibility, parents hope to see them act responsibly.

But fear convinces many teens to hide their emotions. Their fear is that allowing adults to intervene in their decisions will open them to unwanted advice and even criticism. But like a boomerang, fear often returns to the adolescent when he fails to allow for the appropriate intervention his inexperience requires.

Parents May Help Anger Become Deceptive

Despite the fact that young people do not like adult interference as they make choices, we parents tend to give it to them anyway. Our interest in our teen's well-being encourages us to step in when we see a mistake in progress. When Charlie came home from his evening activities, he was greeted by concerned parents. They offered him the opportunity to tell the truth. When it became evident he was not being honest, his mother let loose her frustration by demanding an explanation for his lies.

Notice that Charlie did not answer when his mother asked why he had lied. He retorted, "What difference does it make?" His focus was different from his parents'. While they honed in on his dishonesty, he concentrated on his disgust at having to be accountable to anyone besides himself. Charlie became angry because he felt robbed of his deep need to make his own choices. When the adult's focus runs counter to the teen's, collision is likely.

The teen who makes poor judgment calls obviously needs redirection. Yet, efforts to force responsible choices are stifled when the teen feels resentment. Teenagers like Charlie often refer to parents as "overprotective" or "strict" or "bossy." Parents deny that they are being overly protective. They simply state that they are concerned parents who are trying to teach positive values to their child.

There are several ways parents commonly attempt to redirect teens who have shown poor judgment. They include:

- Checking up on the teen's activities to make sure he is doing what he says he is doing. *"Be sure you tell me exactly where you're going."*
- Offering unsolicited advice. *"If you want to make friends in this world, you had better learn to tell the truth."*
- Punishing the child for his mistake. *"Because you've proven yourself untrustworthy, you're grounded for the weekend."*
- Offering verbal reprimands. *"If you think you can build trust in others by lying, you've got a lot to learn."*
- Demanding a confession. *"Tell us exactly what happened. We have a right to know."*
- Challenging the teen's character. *"It's gotten to the point that we just can't trust you anymore."*

Teenagers do need supervision. Adult advice and even punishment are periodically required. Teens benefit from occasional confrontation. Parents are right in wanting to know the truth about their adolescent's activities. The young person's character needs to be molded. All the responses the parent wants to give the deceptive teen have legitimate concern at their root. However, they provoke an angry teen response, because they clash with the teenager's immediate need.

Remember that one of the teenager's most pressing needs is to feel capable of making his own choices. That need requires attention first. Other needs which are obvious to the parent, but not to the teenager, can be addressed later. The parents can choose to focus on the teen's need for accountability, responsibility, and honesty after they have given his need for independence full attention. Doing so will reduce the teen's urge to react angrily, since his mistakes will have been handled in a way that upholds his dignity.

Offer Help That Will Be Accepted

Because parents want to teach their children to be responsible, it is vital to avoid responses that block the teen from learning. Anger can be a barricade to that learning process. Thus, it makes sense that we look for reactions that will simultaneously keep anger at bay and yet teach the teen to be accountable for acceptable behavior.

Charlie's sister tipped off their parents of his deceitful activity. Of course, they did not like what she told them. They were not especially bothered by the fact that Charlie had spent time with a new girlfriend. That was a normal activity for a teenage boy. They were bothered that he felt compelled to hide his behavior from them. As Mom and Dad discussed how they should correct their son for being dishonest, a good beginning point would have been to consider *why* he had felt the urge to deceive them in the first place.

As we search for solutions to teen problems, we often look at the young person's behavior only from *our* viewpoint. We ignore the teenager's thoughts. Yet, to succeed in answering "why" questions about an adolescent's activities, our richest source of data is in the teen's own mind. While we will not always agree with the teenager's thoughts, understanding them is essential if we are to offer effective guidance. There is a number of reasons Charlie might have lied to his mother as he left the house. He might have

- been embarrassed that his parents would know of his recent interest in a new girlfriend
- hoped to avoid probing questions about his evening activities with Marie
- feared the disapproval of his parents for his choice of girlfriends
- dreaded the likely teasing he could have received from family members
- wanted to wait to announce his new romance until he was more certain of Marie's interest in him
- simply wished to maintain personal privacy

Focusing on the teenager's possible thoughts helps keep parents from feeling personally offended by his deceit. Thinking as the teenager thinks helps parents realize that the teen acted inappropriately, but did not intend to affront them personally. By being objective, parents find themselves able to approach their teenager more calmly. The teenager will notice his parents' lack of judgment and is more likely to show cooperation rather than anger.

Let's change the scene surrounding Charlie's arrival at home.

"Hi, Charlie. Hope you had a good time tonight," his dad said as Charlie walked in.

"Yeah, it was pretty fun."

"Say, Charlie, I know you don't want to hear this, but we heard that you went out with Marie rather than Lance." Dad's facial expression suggested understanding rather than condemnation.

"But Dad, you see . . ." Charlie stammered to find the right words to say.

Interrupting, Dad said, "You don't have to explain things. I know teenagers like to have privacy, especially if it involves a new girl-friend." The look in Dad's eye said, *I understand why you did what you did, even though you know I disapprove of your deceit.*

Charlie looked straight through the floor, feeling foolish for getting caught in a lie. Then his mom asked, "Well Charlie, did you have a good time?"

Lifting his eyes slightly upward Charlie managed a flimsy smile. "Yes. Marie's a nice girl."

"That's good. Let us know when you're going to see her again."

The teenager who left that brief conversation felt considerably less angry than the one who left the first scenario. If anything, any irritation he had would have been directed at himself. With no anger toward his parents to block his thoughts, he is more likely to accept responsibility for his own error.

Charlie's parents made the correct assumption that the young person knew what they expected of him. I can almost see Charlie thinking, *I know my parents don't like it when I tell lies. I need to be more honest.* His parents helped him by eliminating the need to fear them. He was left to think about the reason behind his deception. After thinking, he·could conclude, *I really don't need to hide everything from my parents. They're pretty cool about most things.* That thought is different from the angry feeling, *I can do what I want to do. I don't have to explain myself to anyone!*

There are no guarantees that Charlie will be more honest in the future. The *probability* is higher, though, when parents avoid those comments suggesting anger and judgment. They can safely assume that their teen knows where they stand on the issue of honesty. A simple reminder such as, "Charlie, we expect you to be truthful with us in the future" is all that needs to be said. Charlie can correctly complete his parents' unspoken request. As an added plus, the teen will increase in his maturity and integrity because of his parents' positive management of a potentially explosive situation.

The next time Charlie announces his plans to go out, Mother could say, "I'm trusting you to tell me the truth." There would be no need to offer a verbal reprimand as a forewarning of what might follow if he were again dishonest. Such a word would have dragged up the same fear that provoked his previous deceit and its accompanying anger. A statement of approval could be offered later for being honest. His parents' controlled reaction could help him manage deceitful anger.

CHAPTER NINE

◆

Where's My Sledgehammer?

TEEN ANGER CAN TURN INTO AGGRESSION

Not unlike the riotous behavior experienced by the generation of teenagers in the 1960s and 70s (who are parents today), we are experiencing unsettling violence among today's youth. The intensity of anger in today's teenagers is increasingly frightening. Acting both in gangs and individually, teens are performing heinous acts of force against other teenagers, parents, teachers, even random individuals.

In my work, I see young children who are full of rage even though they have hardly begun to live. You can imagine the size of the emotional powder keg inside these children by the time they reach adolescence. One false assumption is that all angry teens are from lower income, minority, or disadvantaged homes. The appalling truth is that today's teenage violence affects families from all races and social classes. Adolescents from white, black, Hispanic, middle class, upper class, pagan, or Christian homes can be pulled by the same angry magnet that attracts so many to aggression.

Many experts have searched for answers that will stem the national tide of teenage anger. Legislation has been passed to implement government programs aimed at helping youth at risk. Celebrities have criss-crossed the country begging kids to realize the foolishness of their angry urges. Schools have included curriculum hoping to steer children clear of the social potholes that cause emotional wrecks.

Apparently, little has worked. We do not need to abandon the

81

laudable efforts of community leaders, politicians, celebrities, or educators to guide teenagers in a positive direction. But at the root of our national crisis is the need for stronger families. If teenagers are to learn to effectively control their aggressions, the home must be their first classroom.

I have seen teenagers who have committed a variety of aggressive acts. Some are proud of their conquests while others have true remorse. Most will make statements that sound curiously familiar.

- *You have no idea of the fights I've seen in my family.*
- *I get to the point that I just don't care anymore.*
- *Everyone else was doing it. It just got out of hand.*
- *If you're looking for someone to blame, go talk to my parents.*
- *Everyone tells me how bad I am. They're right. I am bad!*
- *What difference does it make? My life's going nowhere anyway.*
- *My friends all turned on me. I had no choice.*
- *I hate life. I hate everything about it!*

Teenagers who are drawn to violence lack a respectable group with whom they can identify. Most have spurned their families, convinced that they will not be nurtured by their parents or siblings. Instead, most of these teens look to their peers for support. Some don't look to anyone at all. All feel isolated in their world of hurt and need.

There is not a single description that fits the families of violent teens. Yet there are two family patterns, which seem to be opposites, that deserve attention. One family type features an overbearing parenting style that pushes the teen to violent rebellion. The other pattern reveals a family life lacking the limits that teaches the teen to consider others' needs. Let's look at each through the eyes of a teen.

CASE STUDY: *A Family at War*

Verne had a vacant look in his eyes. Though just fifteen years old, he had endured more negative experiences than most people twice his age. He wore nice enough clothes and was a handsome, average-sized young man. Even though he spoke in a blunt tone of voice that seethed anger, he managed to be polite. Somewhere along the rough road of his childhood, he had picked up a few manners. Talking openly and with little facial expression, he explained his most recent troubles.

"My mom and my aunt were at my house when I came home. I could tell by the way they were looking at me that they were mad."

"You knew something was up," I asked, "but you didn't quite know what to expect?"

"Oh, I knew what they were thinking. This woman who lives down the street had just called them complaining that I had been riding my moped through her flower bed. Big deal! I squashed a couple flowers. I don't think that's something to get so upset about, do you?"

Wanting to remain neutral on the subject, I responded, "So you had been riding your moped through your neighbor's flower bed and knew that both she and your mother were upset with you, even though you didn't think it was such a big deal. But the minute you saw your mother and aunt, you knew you were in for a fight."

Verne continued. "Yeah. Why does she have to bring my aunt into everything I do, anyway? What's she got to do with it? My mother started accusing me of all this stuff and I didn't feel like taking it off of her, so I turned around to leave."

"And that's when she grabbed you."

"That's when she *hit* me," clarified Verne. "She's always making it sound like it's my fault. She's the one who started all the problems! And then her sister has to jump in and get involved."

"I'm sure you're aware of what your mother's account of the situation is . . ."

Verne interrupted. "Oh yeah. She says I started it. She says I hit her. Well, I did, but what would you do if your mother and her sister jumped on you and tried to drag you back into the room just so they could yell at you even more? They didn't give me any choice!"

"I understand that things just kept getting worse when your stepfather came home."

The youth chuckled sarcastically. "Did my mother tell you what he does when he gets mad? He does what he always does. He pounds me. He calls it a spanking. I call it child abuse. I hate that man. He tells me I can't get away with talking to my mother the way I do, but look at the way he talks to me! He talks even worse to my mother, if you can believe that. And I'm supposed to be this sweet little angel, or else I get busted with his belt." Verne's face was now red with rage. Although he didn't want to cry, he could hardly hold back the tears that had gathered in his eyes.

This teen, now animated, told how his anger had grown throughout his childhood years because of constant fighting in his home. He described his stepfather as an alcoholic ("although he won't admit it") who did little more around the home than make life miserable for everyone else. Verne complained that he got no attention from the man unless it was a reprimand or other, more severe, kinds of punishment. He found himself the constant focus of negative attention. He complained that hardly a day went by that he was not punished. He grumbled, "My stepdad tells me all the time that he's only trying to teach me to act right. I don't want to act right, because I'm not about to give that jerk even a minute of pleasure."

Verne described his mother as a woman whose emotions were in chaos. She had no control over her depression and showed it by being on edge most of the time. Although she was not the driven perfectionist her husband was, she couldn't find many positive comments either. Verne fought her more openly than he fought his stepfather, because he knew he could overpower her emotionally and physically. He claimed he did not like making his mother cry so much, but rationalized his relationship with her. "She's always crying and saying how much she loves me. Sure! If she loves me, why does she act the way she does? I'm always grounded. She's always yelling at me, and then she tells her sister and anyone else who wants to know how bad a son I am."

Before Verne was out of elementary school, he had earned a reputaion as one of the toughest kids in his school. Adults viewed him as a boy with potential who constantly fell short. His peers saw him as a troublemaker and largely avoided him. During his early teen years, Verne began associating with the wrong crowd. Actually, the boys he called his friends were a lot like he was. They were also unhappy and had no one else to turn to (besides other troublemakers) for peer support. Each encouraged the other to rebel. All of them were angry boys looking for someone to accept them.

Verne's friends encouraged him to be violent, if necessary, as a way of gaining control over his corner of the world. By the time he was a teenager, he had learned to force others to answer to his anger by hitting, cursing, or intimidating them. He hoped his aggression would somehow erase his dissatisfaction with life, but his anger only intensified.

CASE STUDY: *"Bad Girl" from a "Perfect" Family*

Janet's family wore a solid gold veneer. Her father and mother had grown up in meager surroundings, but had risen above their humble beginnings to successful positions in life. Janet's father began a career as a plumber and quickly built a large business with over thirty employees. Janet's mother was a partner in the family business and played an important role in its financial success. The family was actively involved in their church and thought of as an example for others to follow. They seemed to have everything going for them.

Janet went through childhood having the best of everything. If she wanted a new toy, her parents bought it. She was given the finest clothes to wear and always looked "perfect." Her friends envied her and often wished they were in her place. Janet had all she needed, except her parents' time and attention.

As a teenager, Janet took advantage of her parents' leniency. Before she was sixteen years old, she habitually stayed out much later than friends her age on weekend nights. She ignored her parents' demands that she quit associating with older teens. She scoffed at the time limits her parents tried to impose on her activities. When she reached that magical sixteenth birthday and was able to drive a car, she was out all hours of the day and night. It seemed she was only home long enough to eat and sleep.

Janet's irresponsibility forced her parents to discipline her more than they had in previous years. Her mother explained, "We gave Janet all the advantages a child could ever hope to have. Then adolescence hit, and she turned into an ungrateful snob."

Janet had seen several counselors. All gave her parents the same directive: *Be more involved in your child's life. You're losing her to a fast-paced peer culture.* To Janet's parents, being involved in their daughter's life meant giving her as much as they could, hoping she would show her appreciation by becoming a compliant child.

Janet knew she was spoiled. "My parents tell people I'm a spoiled brat, but it's their fault. I never asked to be treated that way. If they're going to give me all that stuff, I'll gladly take it. But they had just better not try to get it back, because if they do, they've got a fight on their hands."

Wanting to know more about her fights with her parents, I asked Janet, "Tell me more about these fights. Just how bad are they?"

"How bad? Would you believe my mother, the Sunday school teacher, has hit me and pulled my hair? And my father, the choirboy, has pushed me and threatened to beat me until I can't stand up? That's how bad it is!"

"I'll bet people don't realize all that goes on in your home."

"I doubt it. Everyone thinks we're this perfect family with lots of money. Well, it's not the Brady Bunch around our house. I can tell you that."

Violence had ripped Janet's family apart more than once. Arguments and physical fights over her poor choice of companions, late night hours, drinking, smoking, and abusive language dominated their home atmosphere. Janet's father called the police one night to show her that he would not tolerate her aggressive threats to the family. Janet retaliated by telling the police officer of her parents' neglect. All family members hated their family's lifestyle and desperately wanted to be at peace with one another.

Families in Pain Have Similarities

On the surface it appears that families like Verne's and Janet's have little in common. Verne's family was lower middle class and socially unpolished. Janet's family had all they could want materially and presented themselves quite favorably in the community. Verne's family had been openly belligerent with one another for years. They simply related to one another that way. Janet's family grew into destructive anger only as her parents realized she was taking advantage of their good nature. Verne was aggressive largely because of the way his parents treated him. Janet's parents only became argumentative with their daughter's forceful ways when home life became unbearable.

In both homes several common elements contributed to the violent behavior of their teenagers. They included:

- no appropriate limits and rules to guide the child's behavior
- parental role models that put personal needs or desires above the child's needs
- a scarcity of affirmation that would encourage the teen to cooperate
- a lack of parental priority on family relationships
- a communication style that prevented family members from feeling understood
- parental leadership that failed to teach the teen to be responsible to himself and others

- a home atmosphere in which disagreements were handled with anger

Aggresive teens will often complain loudly about the cards life has dealt them. One teenage boy cried, "I didn't ask to be born to parents who are always putting me down and hurting me!" A pushy girl moaned, "How can I help it if my mother got pregnant when she was seventeen? Why do I have to suffer because she never had time to grow up?" The words of these youth hurt, partly because their sentiments are true. Despite the genuine despair of these youth, we cannot write them off as failures simply because their first few years have seen so little hope or success. Neither can we throw away all faith in their parents. Positive change is possible in families that have been rocked by these kinds of division.

The Value of the Word No

Words are peculiar. Certain words can trigger a variety of reactions from others. We can overuse a word. We can fail to use words when they are needed. We can use too many words. We can use the wrong words. We can use the right words at the wrong time. One word we parents may not fully understand or appreciate is the word "no."

It is both curious and almost embarrassing that a two-letter word can have such a powerful impact on family life, but "no" can become a dominant force within the home. Verne heard the word "no" too often. Maybe it was sometimes only implied, but the youth felt its impact.

- *No, you may not do things the way you want.*
- *No, I didn't hear what you were trying to communicate.*
- *No, you're not an important person in my eyes.*
- *No, I don't trust you.*
- *No, I don't think you can keep it up.*
- *No, I don't have time for you.*
- *No, I won't stop until I feel you've been sufficiently punished.*

Because Verne heard this pocket-sized word with unnecessary frequency, he entered adolescence with "No" tattooed across his heart. Not only did his behavior say *I believe I am of no value as a person*, he also communicated, *There is no way I will cooperate in life.* This high-powered word had a different effect on Janet. Because she heard it infrequently during her childhood, it lost its value amid the sea of other words that swallowed her. Nonetheless, the word "no" impacted her as well.

- *No, the rules do not apply to you.*
- *No, you don't have to endure the same hardships as others.*
- *No, relationships are not as important as material gain.*
- *No, we won't stand in your way.*
- *No, you won't be burdened with consequences for your mistakes.*
- *No, we won't talk about our feelings to one another.*
- *No, there are no boundaries placed on the way you express yourself.*

Although they heard the word "no" in different contexts, its misuse in both families encouraged them to rebel using uncontrolled anger. When "no" is spoken too frequently, the teen becomes resentful and acts out anger through aggression. His hope is that "no" will change to "yes." His violent anger is a statement of despair.

The teen who does not hear "no" often enough pushes the family's patience to the limit. When the teenager forces her parents to include this word in the family vocabulary, the result is an angry explosion. The teen's anger is a payback for all the times she had no boundaries during her youth.

Teach the Value of the Word Yes

Words need to be balanced. In the Old Testament book of Ecclesiastes, the writer relates how confused and hurting individuals view life as futile. The well-known third chapter of this book details the order of our world. (I would encourage you to read this chapter.) All things are balanced. We were not placed in a world with no structure or regularity. There is a time and place for everything. A life with balance and control is a life that has meaning. An unbalanced life is dark, dreary, and full of anger.

If we are to live balanced lives, we should give our children balanced words. Young people seek purpose in life from a variety of sources. A task of the parent is to offer young people boundaries that help them discover their significance. "No" needs to be balanced by the word "yes."

For a boy like Verne, "yes" lets him know he has a place of importance in his family. This same word signals to a girl like Janet that she should share her world with others. Both teenagers can learn:

- *Yes, what you say is important.*
- *Yes, I will listen when you attempt to communicate with me.*
- *Yes, I will try to give you experiences that lead to success.*
- *Yes, I will tell you I love you.*
- *Yes, I will remember that you want to be respected.*
- *Yes, I will refrain from words that stab you in the heart.*
- *Yes, we will laugh together whenever life is fun.*
- *Yes, I will offer boundaries to make your world predictable.*
- *Yes, time will be allowed for you to heal.*

A hopeful teenager has little use for violent anger. Life is not intended to be bland and tasteless, especially to a child or teenager. Hope comes to families who balance the words they give their child. Parents can lead teens to discover the meaning life can have beyond the trivial demands of day-to-day existence. Explosive anger clouds that meaning, leaving the family in despair. Though opposites, both "no" and "yes" need to be part of the teen's family vocabulary.

—◆—

CHAPTER TEN

Anger That Stands Still

STUBBORN ANGER CAN HAVE AGGRESSIVE ROOTS

Anger cannot be ignored. Certainly parents would *like* to ignore their children's anger, but they *can't*. Anger is stubborn. We sometimes assume that teenagers enjoy being angry. The truth is that they, too, would like to ignore it. I have heard many teens say things like, "I wish I weren't angry all the time. I hate feeling this way!" Like their parents, they would enjoy the peace that comes from life without excessive anger.

Some teenagers try hard to block their anger by concealing it from others. Still others recognize their anger but use it as a silent weapon. Anger can go underground as the teenager plays stubborn games with his emotions.

Even young children observe how anger is handled in their home. Their early family interaction teaches them how to express this emotion and use it to their advantage. Some learn to explode with rage, blowing everyone down in the process. Others stubbornly stand by their anger, daring others to try and get by it. But even a young child can use anger to resist a parent's authority. By the time adolescence comes around, the teenager has usually mastered the way he expresses anger.

CASE STUDY: *Martha's Anger Digs In*

Mr. Upton shook his head slowly as a knowing smile slid across his face. "People don't believe me when I tell them what Martha is really like. Almost everyone who knows her sees a kind, sweet-natured fourteen-year-old. A number of people have said to me that they wish their teenager were as easy to handle as Martha seems to be. If they only knew what they were asking for." Mr. Upton shook his head as he spoke.

This dad gave an example of his daughter's stubbornness. "When she was two years old, we had a rough time potty training her. We knew she was ready to be trained, but she was pretty headstrong. One Saturday afternoon I told Martha and her brother I would take them swimming. Of course they both wanted to go. As they were getting their swimming suits on, I just routinely mentioned that they needed to use the bathroom before we went to the pool. Martha hadn't been since she got up that morning, so I knew she needed to go.

"In her typical way, Martha refused. She said she didn't need to use the bathroom. I knew her bladder must have been about ready to burst and told her she couldn't go with us if she wouldn't do what I told her. I was pretty upset with her because she was being stubborn for no reason. Well, Martha never said a word, but it was obvious I couldn't make her do what I wanted her to do. Cathy stayed home with Martha while I took Shane to the swimming pool. Cathy convinced me that I needed to stick to my word if I had told Martha she couldn't go swimming.

"When Shane and I left, Martha was sitting on the potty with a bullheaded look on her face. I told her that I was taking her brother swimming and that I was sorry she had chosen to stay home. She knew I was mad at her. Before I left, I informed her that she could not get off the potty until she had used it. She never said a word to me. Even though she was just two years old, she had a way of staring a hole right through a brick wall.

"Shane and I came home about two hours later. When I came into the house, Martha was sitting in my bedroom just as happy as she could be. I thought, *I'm glad she's not still hanging on to the anger she had when I left her.* Cathy motioned me into another room so she could fill me in on what had just happened. She told me that the entire time I was gone Martha sat on the potty and refused to use it. The split second she heard my car pull into the driveway, she did her business, hopped off the commode, flushed, and ran to the chair in our bedroom so that when I saw her, she could give me a broad smile. She didn't want to give me the pleasure of thinking I had caused her any discomfort while I was gone! And things haven't changed a bit since then."

Stubborn Anger Invites Power Struggles

By age fourteen Martha was a master at using her stubborn anger as a manipulative weapon. She had learned that her unspoken anger could be parleyed into a negotiating tool. When she wanted things her way she could make silent but emphatic demands.

Recognizing the purpose of anger helps teenagers deal with that emotion. There is a reason behind every behavior and emotion a young person displays. Discovering its purpose makes stubborn anger easier to accept and manage. Here's what teenagers say when asked to justify reasons for their stubborn anger:

- *I want to show my parents I'm upset, but I don't want to yell and scream because they'll think I'm out of control.*
- *If I say what I'm feeling, I probably won't be understood.*
- *I like to do things that irritate my parents, but when they accuse me of being angry, I can deny that I really am.*
- *I don't know how to put my feelings into words. When I feel something real strong, I just can't give in.*
- *If my parents want something from me and I quietly refuse to cooperate, it drives them crazy!*
- *Sometimes I can't get rid of my anger, but I just don't feel like talking about it.*

- *Holding my anger in is one of the best ways to get back at my parents. They don't know what I'm thinking.*

With each of these statements the teenager hopes to maintain some semblance of control over his world. Adamant refusal to be open with anger is a powerful way the teen can create tension with parents. We parents usually do not like having to deal with a silent, angry adolescent. Their tight control over their emotions causes *us* to feel out of control! A vicious cycle of struggling between parent and teen can whirl a family into constant disruption.

In Martha's case, I learned that she was fairly talented as a musician. She had taken piano lessons since the age of seven and had made significant progress. After the novelty of playing the piano wore off, practicing became a chore for Martha. Using a variety of coercive tactics, her parents usually managed to see that she was prepared for her weekly lessons.

Now in high school, Martha privately decided she had taken piano lessons long enough. She was on the school track team and wanted to focus on running instead of playing the piano. When the time came to arrange Martha's fall schedule, a showdown between Martha and her parents quickly became obvious.

Martha's parents asked her to join them in the living room one evening to discuss their dilemma. Mom spoke up first. "Martha, I need to call Mrs. McCall to talk with her about your piano schedule this year. What do you think I should tell her? Do you want your lessons on Tuesday like last year?"

Stone silence. Martha sat still, staring at nothing in particular. The silence that lasted only a few seconds seemed like years. The Upton family had been through this scene before. The conversation may have been different, but the backdrop was uncomfortably familiar. Each parent was thinking in tandem, *Oh no, not again. Please, Martha, don't do this to us. Make it simple on all of us, and give us a quick and easy decision.*

Though Martha was motionless and speechless, her mind was also working overtime. *I'm not about to take piano lessons again this year. I've told them already I'm running track in high school, and I can't do that and take piano lessons at the same time. If they can't get that message through their thick skulls, I'll just have to force it on them. I'm not giving in!*

Dad broke the stiff silence. "Well, Martha. Are you going to answer your mother? She needs to call Mrs. McCall tonight. What day will work out best for you to take piano lessons this year?"

Another long, hard pause followed. Finally Martha summoned her courage and said, "I'm not taking piano lessons anymore. Tell Mrs. McCall she can put someone else in my old time slot. I want to run track this year, and to be good at it I need to work out all year. I won't have time to practice the piano."

Reasoning with their stubborn daughter, Mom urged Martha, "Be sensible about this, Martha. You can play piano *and* run. You managed to do both last year. I don't see any reason you can't do it again. We can make it work. Let's give it a try. You're so good on the piano, I'd hate to see you give it up." Both parents watched nervously for their daughter's reaction. She merely raised her eyebrows slightly and cocked her head as if to say, *Go ahead and make whatever plans you want, but my mind is made up.*

Let's stop and examine how Martha used her stubbornness to draw her parents into a power struggle. A problem had presented itself: a decision needed to be made about Martha's piano lessons. Her parents hoped to encourage a stubborn daughter to continue studying piano. Martha viewed the situation differently. Sure, she was concerned about whether or not she would have to take piano lessons, but she was more concerned about the issue of control. She wanted command of the decisions that directly involved her. She had reached a point in her life where she wanted personal authority over her activities. The struggle between Martha and her parents was over control, not piano lessons.

Teenagers Choose the Anger That Suits Their Needs

Teens realize there is more than one way to express their views forcefully. They can growl their angry messages or be overpowering as they force their anger on others. Or they can subtly, silently strongarm those standing in their way. Martha used few words to show her anger, but did it in a way that could hardly be ignored. From her perspective, she was not without options as she negotiated with her parents:

- refuse to speak, forcing her parents to decide just how far they were willing to press the issue
- agree to a day that she could take her lessons, but refuse to practice as required
- take her piano lessons, but purposely do poorly, thus seducing her teacher to suggest that she be allowed to quit
- allow her parents to arrange a lesson date, but refuse to get out of the car when her parent dropped her off at the teacher's studio
- give in to her parents' wishes and be a compliant, but disgruntled, daughter

Likewise, Mr. and Mrs. Upton had several options of responding to their daughter's mulish anger. They could:

- use parental authority to make the decision they thought was best and prepare for the inevitable onslaught that would follow
- make the decision they thought was in Martha's best interest, but then choose not to fight her if she dug in her heals
- allow Martha to call the shots, even though she might make a mistake
- try to force Martha into calling her piano teacher, hoping that by putting the burden of responsibility on her she would give in to their wishes

As we look at these choices, there clearly is no simple solution to the struggle. The only appropriate answer to the Uptons' problem begins with that fainthearted phrase "it depends."

It depends on the parents' willingness to slug it out with the daughter—one more time.

- It depends on just how mistaken they believe it would be for Martha to quit piano in favor of running track.
- It depends on how closely tied to her self-esteem they think a new activity would be to Martha.
- It depends on how badly they want to avoid being "weaklings" by letting Martha have her way.
- It depends on how strongly they fear a "ripple effect" in which Martha would stubbornly insist on a series of changes.

Martha's parents decided to sidestep the almost certain battle over piano lessons. They feared it would interfere with their relationship with her. They allowed her to drop piano in favor of running on the school track team. Of course, Martha was delighted she had "won" the battle over piano lessons. Actually, the whole family won since Martha's anger had been silenced.

The Question of Control Remains

It is possible to lose a battle with an angry teenager and still win the war of household control. The parent's emotional reaction will determine how the teen uses stubborn anger in the future. The teen is certain to note how her parents handled the emotional crisis. When the parents announce their decisions, the teenager is more interested in their *emotion* than in their decision. Of course, she cares about the decision, but she cares more about the underlying emotional tug-of-war.

Again, there were several options the Uptons could have chosen as they decided how to handle the situation. They could have:

- sternly told her she could choose between piano lessons and running track, but then dared her to go against their wishes
- emotionally appealed to her to stick with piano lessons and then given up in exasperation when it became evident she would not cooperate
- thrown up their hands in defeat screaming, "Forget it! You're impossible to reason with. Just do what you want to do. We don't care!"
- told her she could decide which activity she would choose, but then questioned her decision by stating, "Martha, you're making a big mistake. I hope you realize that. But, we're washing our hands of this whole thing. It's your blunder, not ours."
- explained Martha's options to her and then accept, without immediate comment, the choice she made

The Uptons chose the last of these options. There was no magic in their decision. What made their choice successful was their straight-forwardness in communicating it to Martha. When Martha saw that her parents were comfortable making a difficult choice, she knew she had less room to manipulate them in the future.

A teen who recognizes that her stubborn anger creates tension in her parents will repeatedly use it as an emotional battering ram. Teenagers study their parents' emotional reactions as family decisions are made. A decision announced passionately sends the message: *I'm giving in to your stubbornness, but I don't like being held hostage by your anger.* Decisons that are communicated calmly suggest: *I'm making a choice that I can live with. Your anger has a limited influence on how I conduct myself.*

A teenager who wants to control the household will use anything that works to emotionally imprison parents. Parents who wish to keep control of the home must first control their own anger. Doing so sends a potent message to the teen: *Our main concern is for the emotional health of our family. We assume you know our feelings on the matter, so we will not get into an emotional shoving match with you.* This is how Martha's parents resolved the showdown with their daughter. They prevented Martha from using the most powerful weapon she possessed to seize control of the home: *their emotions.*

Anger cannot be ignored. Neither the parent nor the teenager can make it disappear by wishing. Rather than close our eyes to stubborn anger, we must confront it without flinching. Such anger does not have to grip the family. Teens can be taught to use anger in a healthy way without letting it force stubborn family feuds. As parents control their anger, they decrease the likelihood of the kinds of emotional brawls that throw the family into conflict. Parental control over anger keeps family leadership in its rightful place—with the parent.

◆

CHAPTER ELEVEN

Anger with a Smile!

A LOOK AT PASSIVE-AGGRESSIVE ANGER

A friend once asked, "Just what is passive-aggressive anger?" Sometimes answers can best be given in story form.

A long-suffering woman had been married for years to a man who could only be described as gruff and inconsiderate. This man grumbled, griped, and complained about everything she did. His wife couldn't do anything right in his eyes.

One of the woman's friends was familiar with the situation and marveled that she could endure her husband's eternal foul mood. One day the friend questioned the source of this lady's patience by asking, "How do you live with the resentment that surely must eat away at you? Your husband never says a kind word to you and yet you roll along in life with a smile on your face and a song in your heart. How do you do it?"

Shyly the woman leaned toward her friend and revealed the secret of her sanity. "You're right, my husband rarely says a kind word to me and he's seldom in a pleasant mood, but I have a way to quietly rid myself of my anger toward him. You see, every Tuesday and Friday after he has gone to work, I use his toothbrush to clean the toilet bowl and then put it back in its place for him to use that night. Even though he doesn't know what I've done, I feel as if I've gotten even with him." That's passive-aggressive anger: an anger expressed so subtly that others are scarcely aware of it!

Teens do not need to rant and rave to show their anger. Some, like the wife in this story, get even quietly, privately. A victim of passive anger may be unaware how upset the young person really is—that's how much a secret this type of anger can be. This anger is passive because of the docile, almost unnoticed way it seeps out of an individual. It is called aggressive, though, because its aim is to send a powerful message: *I'm losing control of my world and want to gain it back!*

Most passive-aggressive teens are otherwise compliant. The teen's desire to avoid the tag of "troublemaker" pushes him to hide his anger. By refraining from boisterous, offensive anger, the compliant teen can deny ownership of this disturbing emotion if confronted. In this sense, passive-aggressive anger can damage the teen and his family as much as outwardly aggressive anger, because it is never dealt with straightforwardly.

Case Study: *Brent's Disguised Anger*

"Brent never gave me a minute's trouble until the last few months. He's still a good boy, but I don't know what's wrong with him. I can't make him do anything for me any more. I ask him to do something simple, like clean up his bathroom, and he works just a few minutes and quits. I'll ask him to come back and finish the job he started, and he always minds me. But when I turn my back on him, he quits working again. He's that way about everything! I just can't get him to follow through on the jobs he has to do. I don't know why he's this way. When I talk to him about his behavior, he seems to feel genuinely sorry, but things don't change."

Mrs. Mosby never dreamed she would be confronted with a problem teenager. Life had not been easy for her and her family, but through all the hardships, they had somehow managed to stick together. She felt delight that her two children, and especially Brent, seemed unscathed by a home life that lacked what other families had. A single mother, Mrs. Mosby had worked hard to provide for her boys. Brent never complained that he had less than his friends, even though he secretly wished for an easier lifestyle.

I found Brent to be just as easygoing as his mother claimed. He was intent on making a good impression. But when the subject of his failed responsibility arose, he seemed hurt. "I don't want you to think that I don't care," he said. He obviously wanted me to think highly of him. But he added, "I know I disappoint my mother, and I don't like it. But, I just can't tell her some of the things I feel."

Trying to grasp what Brent meant, I asked for clarification. "You mean she doesn't listen when you try to let her know how you feel about things?"

Brent squirmed in his seat, searching for the right way to say what he thought. He didn't dare suggest he was angry at his mother, even though he was. "Well, kind of. She listens to me, but I don't think she knows what I mean. She makes too many decisions for me. It just drives me crazy." Brent cast his eyes down, unsure of what I thought of him.

Trying to look at matters as Brent did, I said, "I guess she means well, but she comes across as trying to do too much for you."

That comment struck a chord with Brent. "Yeah! That's it. She's overprotective." As soon as he spoke, a guilty look ran across his face. A silent message shot from his eyes, *I feel bad whenever I voice my anger aloud. I'm not supposed to say negative things about others, especially my mother, because I know children are expected to honor their parents.*

Brent was deceived by his own sensitivity! He had come to believe that there was no place in his world for "negative" emotions. For him to be all he thought was expected of him, he felt he should keep his negative thoughts to himself.

Brent changed looks, but was still uncomfortable as I said, "You know, Brent, even when we try *not* to say negative things, we usually show our emotions anyway." Brent was puzzled, but strained to listen. "If our emotions can't be expressed in words, we show them through our behavior. One way or another, our feelings come out."

Brent was curious to know more. He tilted his head, drew his eyebrows in, and asked, "You mean you think *I'm* angry?"

Smiling at Brent, I answered, "I'll bet that when you only do half of what your mother asks you to do you're telling her, 'Mom, I don't like these silly jobs. Why can't you get someone else to do it, or at least pay me for doing it?'"

Brent looked as if his hand had been caught in a cookie jar. He sheepishly smiled and let go with an unconvincing chuckle. Nodding his head, he simply muttered, "Yeah." He could not, or would not, elaborate because the guilt of talking openly about his passive style of anger would have made a knot in his stomach.

Passive-Aggressive Anger and Control

Let's return to a point made a few pages back. Despite its quiet nature, passive-aggressive anger sends the message, *I'm losing control of my world, and I want to gain it back!* All children, regardless of their age, want to be in control of their lives. A compliant teenager, like Brent, may temporarily relinquish control to a parent because he wants so badly to please that adult. Yet as time passes and the young person wants more freedom, he may engage in a seemingly uncharacteristic struggle for control. Some teenagers grab for control openly and emphatically. But the passive teen tries, usually unsuccessfully, to politely wrestle control from his parent. But because this otherwise compliant teenager masks his anger beneath a pleasant facade, family communication fails. His anger still festers while his parent is confused by this voiceless emotion.

Searching for some way to control his world, the passive-aggressive teen turns to subtle emotional expressions. He desperately hopes his passive communication will speak his feelings to others. Yet, his communication lacks honesty. Fear allows the teen to send to others only partial messages. His faint hope is that others will read between the lines of his communication and give him control of his life again.

Brent wanted to tell his mother, "Let me have more independence. I think I can decide what kind of person I want to be." But instead of openly voicing this message, he disguised it through passive rebellion. His passive behaviors included:

- Only partially completing assigned tasks. *(I would rather make my own decisions about what I will do.)*
- Doing as little as possible to fulfill an obligation. *(I'm irritated by your protective stance over me. If I show you that I can't be counted on, maybe you'll leave me alone.)*
- Agreeing too quickly with others' criticism. *(I'm frustrated that you didn't catch the real message I'm sending, but I'm too timid to speak up.)*
- Pleading ignorance when confronted. *(If I act like I don't know what you're talking about, you can't get angry with me. That way, I can continue to do as I please.)*
- "Accidentally" forgetting to complete a responsibility. *(I don't have the same priorities as you do. I would rather decide for myself what I will do.)*
- Offering a weak apology for irresponsible behavior. *(I'll say what I have to say to maintain my positive reputation, but I'm really not sorry for what I did.)*

All these unspoken communications were control tactics. His maneuvers failed him, though, because others missed his intended message. Brent wanted to tell his mother what he really felt, but worried that if he did, he would lose his good standing in the family. Instead, he sent silent signals with the slim chance that they would be received. He suffered growing frustration, and its related anger, when his passive hints went unnoticed.

Who Controls the Dialogue in the Home?

Brent's mother talked of how she had tried to rechannel her son's growing irresponsibility. "I have to admit that nothing I've done has worked. Every time I try to help Brent, things only seem to get worse."

"There's probably a reason Brent reacts like he does," I said.

Mrs. Mosby agreed there had to be a reason for her son's behavior, but could not identify it. "I've tried to think of why he is so lethargic when I'm only trying to help, but I haven't found the answer yet. What do you think?"

I asked Mrs. Mosby to look with me at the silent messages beneath Brent's behavior. As she saw for the first time what he wanted to communicate, she was almost embarrassed. "Now I can see why he does some of the things he does. It makes sense! No wonder he won't talk to me. He probably thinks I won't understand, so he won't take the risk of saying what he really thinks."

Mrs. Mosby then described her typical response to Brent—the ones that created communication barriers:

- Forcing decisions on Brent rather than allowing him to come to his own conclusions. *"Let me tell you what you should have done to make sure you would be successful."*
- Reasoning with Brent, hoping he would see her point of view. *"If you would only listen to me, I could help you. I've been around a lot longer than you have, you know."*
- Keeping Brent from making mistakes from which he would profit. *"I won't let you have a voice in what happens to you. If I did, you'd only mess things up. Let me decide what's best for you."*
- Rejecting Brent's opinions because he was too young to make responsible judgments. *"I know that's what you think, but how can a teenager know what's best?"*
- Offering quick criticism without recognizing any of the teen's positive accomplishments. *"Your bathroom is filthy! How can you stand to go in there?"*

By making statements like these, Mrs. Mosby was attempting to force control on her unreliable son. Her intent was to teach responsibility to Brent. Despite her best efforts, though, matters only got worse! Instead of becoming *more* reliable, he became *less* reliable. Who was controlling the home? Brent!

By refusing to respond openly to his mother, Brent continued to hammer away his silent messages. He closed the door on open dialogue with his mother. His smoldering anger tiptoed into the forefront of family life. Though it was barely recognizable, passive-aggressive anger dominated the home atmosphere.

Bring Out the Unspoken Dialogue

Until a passive teenager feels his emotions are both accepted and understood, his anger will dominate the home. Maybe the look on his face is pleasant, but anger drives his behavior. Bringing his resentment to the surface not only relieves the teenager, it lets the family move past the teen's angry feelings. In their place, positive feelings of acceptance and satisfaction can surround the teen.

Brent's mother was better prepared the next time he displayed passive aggression. One evening when she had to leave the house for a short time, Mother asked Brent and his brother to take care of a few housekeeping chores. Brent balked, saying he had planned to have a friend come over to listen to a new tape. Mother reacted to Brent's mild protest saying, "I don't mind if Tony comes over. Just make sure you do your chores while I'm gone." Brent only heard that Tony could come over and privately thought he could delay his responsibilities.

When Mother arrived home a short time later, she saw that her older son had done his chores to satisfaction. Brent, however, had virtually ignored his jobs. Although her first impulse was to confront Brent's irresponsibility, she refrained. Calling Brent aside she observed, "You didn't get your jobs done. I'm sure you were more interested in spending time with Tony than in working around the house."

Brent felt the need to account for his noncompliance. "Oh yeah. Well, Tony got here sooner than I thought he would, so I didn't have a chance to finish." He smiled at his mom, hoping to win her pardon.

Mother ignored his limp excuse but commented on what she knew to be Brent's feelings. "Doing chores isn't your favorite thing to do, especially when you have a friend over." Brent readily agreed by shaking his head. "And yet, I want you to do what I've asked. I need your help keeping things neat around here. I'll have to ask you to go ahead and finish your jobs."

"Now?"

Mom nodded her head and turned to walk away.

Brent called her back saying, "But Mom! Tony's still here!"

"You have your jobs to do. Tony doesn't have to leave." Without further comment she went about her own activities while Brent did what he had to do, angry that his mother had imposed her rules on him.

Later in the evening Mother found Brent alone in his room. Though he was brooding, he was not as upset then as when he had been told to do his chores. Sitting down near Brent, she said, "You were pretty upset that I asked you to finish your jobs while Tony was still here."

Brent said nothing, but gave a slight nod that she was right. Not sure how to respond to his mother's comment, he remained silent. After a brief moment, Mother continued to focus on her son's feelings. "When there are things you want to do but you have to do other things that aren't nearly as enjoyable, it's tempting to ignore your job. But I expect you to take care of your chores." She wore a warm expression on her face as she spoke. She remembered what it was like to be a carefree teenager. Brent remained silent, but somehow felt the tension inside himself being released. It was nice to hear his mother say that she understood his feelings. A thin smile was all he could muster, but it was genuine. He was not merely trying to force a pleasant look to hide his anger. The contentment on his face resulted from feeling understood.

As Mother stood up to leave, she reached out and pinched Brent on the arm. "Thanks for doing your work even though you didn't want to. You did a good job!"

Not only did Mrs. Mosby feel she had released the tension in the home, she felt in control of the home atmosphere. A few days later she looked back on her experience and evaluated her dialogue with Brent. "In the past I would have gotten mad at Brent when I came in the house and saw that his chores were still undone. I would have felt obligated to talk with him about why I was upset that he had not done what he was supposed to do. I think it took Brent by surprise when I just told him what I expected and left it at that. I don't think he was prepared when I came into his room later that night to let him know I understood why he had made the choices he made. He probably expected a lecture on being more responsible."

Because Mrs. Mosby had effectively broken through Brent's passive anger, the teenager was free to draw these conclusions about his dealings with his mom:

- *Mom is capable of looking at things the way I do. Maybe I can start being more open with her about the way I feel.*
- *I guess I should do what I'm asked to do when I'm asked to do it. I can avoid unwanted confrontations that way.*
- *Maybe Mom's not so overprotective. She's not trying to tell me how I should act or what I should feel.*
- *If Mom is willing to listen to me, I can risk being more honest with her.*

Conversations that fail to acknowledge the teenager's thoughts and feelings encourage anger to go underground. Not all teenagers feel comfortable expressing their emotions forcefully. Some hide behind the passive mask of an anger that drives a wedge between themselves and others. Parents who talk openly with their teenager make it easier for the teen to reveal his true feelings. Once anger is coaxed from hiding it can be dealt with more effectively. The quiet destruction of passive anger can be avoided.

CHAPTER TWELVE

◆

Who Can Find the Teen's Anger?

ANGER CAN BE THE DRIVE BEHIND DEPRESSION

Teen depression is on the rise. For years public consensus held that teenagers were not old enough to be depressed! Depression was a disorder reserved for adulthood. We need only look at the steady rise of teenage suicide over the past thirty years to be convinced that more teens than ever are unsure of their life's worth. Although teenage depression isn't identical to the adult version, similar feelings of despair are evident in both groups. Many teenagers use their anger as a way of stating just how depressing life is to them. Depressed teenagers say things such as:

- *Life just doesn't matter anymore.*
- *I'm ready to check it in. Nothing ever works out for me.*
- *Does anybody know I'm alive? I feel so lonely.*
- *People are going to hear me out even if I have to get in their face and force them to listen!*
- *My parents try to put words in my mouth. I can't say what I really feel.*
- *I feel like crying, but when I try to, the tears won't come. It's like I'm almost dead.*
- *No matter what anybody tries to do to help me, it's too late. Things have been bad so long, life can't get better.*

Such thoughts and emotions are in full fury in many adolescent minds even though they were once considered adult issues. Most of

111

these teens feel as though they *cannot* solve their problems, and they have faint hope that others can provide the answers they are looking for. Depressed teenagers almost always trace their despair to failed relationships, frequently within the home. Uncertain family relationships can spin off of other personal problems. Beneath the depression lies a bundle of uncertain angry feelings.

Teenagers are famous for acting out their depression through their behavior. Careful observation of a teenager may give the first hint that anger has turned into depression. Here are some of the major symptoms of teenage depression:

- complaints of low self-esteem
- diminished appetite or increased appetite
- unusual sleep patterns (too much or too little sleep)
- moodiness; irritability
- low energy or weak motivation
- weak concentration
- negative view of things
- feelings of despair or hopelessness
- social isolation or withdrawal
- chronic complaints or pessimism
- increased risk taking
- comments about death and dying

Depressed Teens Feel Rejected

One depressed girl continually voiced the feeling that she had been rejected throughout her childhood. When I asked her to tell about how she had been rejected, she laughed sarcastically. Hurt was painted on her face. "Do you have some time? We may be here all afternoon. It'll take me a while to tell it all." A teenager may feel rejected by her parents when the adult:

- places a greater priority on work than on family relationships
- discounts the importance of the teenager's point of view

- ignores the teen's continuing need to be touched in a loving way
- shouts and yells to get a point across to a stubborn youth
- talks negatively about the teen to others
- punishes more than encourages
- argues constantly with a spouse without regard to its effect on the teenager
- offers abundant criticism but scant affirmation

CASE STUDY: *Rachel's Depression*

Rachel wondered why her life had not been as easy as that of most of her friends. Nothing about her childhood seemed to have been normal. During her fifteen years, Rachel and her family had lived in eight different towns, making it impossible for her to groom the friendships she so badly desired. Her mother had been through two unhappy marriages and was in a third marriage that seemed no different from the others. Rachel did not really know her father. He'd left the home when she was six years old. She visited him periodically, but since he lived in a different town it was hard for them to get together. Besides, her father seemed disinterested in parenthood.

Rachel hated the word "stepparent." She had lived with two stepfathers and did not like either of them. Her first stepfather had tried to touch her in places he had no business touching. The other constantly encouraged her mother to punish her for a "bad attitude." Rachel was forever mad at her mother for ignoring the way these men mistreated her. It seemed she didn't care.

"I've got a bad attitude all right, but I'm not the only one in our house who does," Rachel defensively admitted. "My brother has a worse attitude problem than I do, but he never gets punished like I do. They say that because I'm a girl, I can't do the things he gets to do. Right! When a boy does something wrong, it's no big deal. But let me do the same thing and just watch what happens. I can tell you this—it isn't nice. And look at my mother and stepfather. You talk about a bad attitude—they both have one! They never say anything nice to anybody, especially me."

Rachel's mother and stepfather saw little hope for Rachel. Her mother stated with a sigh, "I had hoped Rachel would turn out better than this. She used to be a pretty good girl, but I have to tell you that I can't wait for her to get old enough to leave the house. It's that bad at home."

Rachel's family never thought she might be depressed. She had been called other things: defiant, stubborn, ungrateful, or unmotivated, but not depressed. Her parents thought that depressed teenagers only sat and stared at the walls all day. Rachel was active and seldom sat still long enough to look at a wall. She certainly did not seem emotionally withdrawn like a depressed person was supposed to be. She let go of her emotions regularly, seldom holding them in.

The Many Faces of Teen Depression

The outward appearance of depression differs in teenagers. Some depressed youth are withdrawn, while others are much more active. Some withhold their thoughts, while others let them go with a vengeance. There is no single descriptive summary that tells what teenage depression looks like. Teenage depression comes in a variety of packages:

- A boy does well in his classes at school, but is a total failure in his social relationships. Although he would like to have more friends, he makes little effort to branch out socially. His belief is that others are surely not likely to embrace him as a part of their group. This young person is too well acquainted with the feeling of loneliness.
- A girl seems to have everything going for her. She lives in the right part of town, wears name brand clothes, knows lots of people, and drives a nice car. Yet, beneath this cloak of personal prosperity lies a gnawing feeling of doubt. This girl has always

felt that she was not quite good enough. Whatever she achieved, or however comfortable her lifestyle, she lacked the personal security that convinced her she was okay. As a way of seeking proof of her worth, she followed the crowd, hoping they could convince her of her value.

- A tough boy struck fear in the minds of many of his peers. Known for his streetwise conduct, this youth was looked upon as a hopeless juvenile delinquent. He had been in more than his share of fights and was known to quickly challenge anyone who tried to show him up. Many saw that this youth was behaviorally troubled, but would not consider him depressed. Yet, in private conversation he confided, "I have to show others I'm tough. If I don't, I've got nothing left. I'm nobody."

I often ask teenagers the question, "Are you depressed?" A surprising number of adolescents will quickly acknowledge, "Yes, all the time." And they are not just casually admitting to the normal frustrations of adolescent life. Though they may fool others by achieving success in school, on the social scene, or even on the streets, teenagers have enough knowledge of themselves to know when something is wrong. And though other depressed teens deny obvious feelings of depression, many will state in their later adult life, "I knew I was depressed when I was younger. I just didn't want to admit it. If I faced up to how bad I felt about myself, I probably couldn't have handled the pain. That's why I told myself and everyone else that I was alright."

Depressed Teens Invite Criticism

Teenagers often have a hard time being open about their depression. After all, one reason for their blue feelings is the inability to honestly express their thoughts and emotions. Teens are infamous for disguising their feelings through other behavioral displays. Although it does not seem that they are trying to draw attention to their feelings, many teenagers will confess that beneath their behavior is a message crying to be heard: *"I'm hurting! Will someone please recognize my need and offer me some relief?"*

On one of the rare evenings that Rachel sat down at the dinner table with her family, her mother broached the subject of her unwillingness to associate with the family. "Rachel, why don't you ask some of your friends to come over to our house? You're always going over to someone else's house. We really don't know your friends very well."

Rachel immediately recoiled. "Are you kidding? Bring my friends over here? That's a real joke! No way!"

Rachel's stepfather was instantly offended. He had no intention of allowing a teenaged girl to speak so rudely in his presence, especially when the clear implication was that she had no respect for him or his wife. "Hey! Let me tell you something, Miss Smart Mouth. If you don't think we're good enough for you, you can just keep right on walking when you go out that front door. Your mother was just asking you to let us meet some of those punks you hang out with. There's nothing wrong with that, is there? Or are you ashamed of your friends and don't want us to see them?"

Rachel's blood pressure rose quickly. As her stepfather talked, she thought to herself, *That's the very reason I don't want any of my friends to come over here. I'm so embarrassed at the way people talk to one another around here, there's no way I'm going to let them see firsthand how badly I'm treated. I couldn't stand the humiliation.*

Not knowing how to say what she felt, Rachel simply exploded, "What did I do to deserve this? You want me to leave? I'd love to leave this hellhole! And I'm going to as soon as I'm old enough to pay my way and live on my own. And when I do, you won't have to worry about me getting in your way anymore because I'll never step foot in this house again. I promise you'll never see me. I hate this place!"

Rachel's mother was floored and had no idea what she should

do. She knew her husband had spoken too harshly, but she couldn't allow Rachel to scream at him the way she had. She felt a need to regain control of a daughter she feared she could hardly restrain. In addition to her fear, she was also angry that her child would act so ugly toward her husband.

Using the best judgment she could find in the heat of battle, Mother quickly tried to break up an inevitable war between her daughter and husband. "Both of you, stop! We can't talk that way. Rachel, just go to your room. And stay there the rest of the night. You can't go anywhere with that attitude."

Rachel picked up a bottle of ketchup and slung it across the table, narrowly missing her brother's head. "That's fine! I don't want to sit in here with a bunch of pigs anyway!" As she headed out of the kitchen, she defiantly screamed, "And you can't keep me home tonight. I'm going out!"

With Rachel out of the kitchen, the stepfather mumbled to his wife, "You're gonna have to do something about that kid. She's getting out of hand."

The angry mother snapped back, "Oh, shut up! You're just as much at fault as she is."

Listen to the Message of Depression

Though it is difficult to do, the most healing response parents can offer when anger disrupts the home is to focus on the underlying messages beneath that emotion. For a moment, the angry reactions of the teen need to be set aside. Remember, there is a reason for every behavior and emotion shown by the adolescent. By understanding the origin of the anger, the depression, and their accompanying fireworks, parents are in a much better position to regain leadership in the family. The parent needs to start the change cycle, for it is the parent who has the greater degree of life experience and wisdom.

Rachel's actions screamed for understanding. Many hidden comments accompanied her angry explosion, including:

- *I feel that my family does not like me or accept me.*
- *I would like to run away from it all and make a new life for myself.*
- *Life in this family has been unfair to me.*
- *I'm becoming increasingly convinced that nothing I do will make things better, so why should I try?*
- *I'm all alone with my thoughts and emotions, and I don't know how to handle them.*
- *No one in my family understands me, so why should I trust that anyone else can?*

Viewing a teenager's anger from her eyes sheds a strange, even unfamiliar, light on the problems depressed behavior brings into the home. Of course, the parent will not agree with all the opinions of the teenager. Simply understanding the adolescent's point of view, though, puts the adult in a better position to respond in a helpful way. Looking at Rachel's behavior in this way, we can generate several ways her needs could be addressed. Her parents could take the edge off her angry depression by:

- Avoiding comments that put her on the defensive. Challenging the logic of her choices will push her to express her needs more forcefully. A cooperative spirit is the last thing a berated teen will develop. Teens who have been put on the defensive tend to overstate their anger to make sure it is heard.
- Waiting until her emotions are past to make critical comments. Helpful tips on getting along with others are much better received when the teen's emotions are stable rather than volatile. Parents may use the right words, but say them at the wrong time. The result will be increased teen anger.

- Showing an interest in her world. When parents approach the teenager with a desire to know more about her interests, the teen will feel more comfortable with her role in the family. She will want to become a part of the family.
- Modeling the kind of emotional control we hope to see the teen display. When our words say, "Control your anger" but our behavior says, "I'm not in control of my emotions," the teen will pay closer attention to the second message than the first. She will likely respond with behavior similar to the adult's.

But What about Discipline?

Rachel's mother agreed that she needed to concentrate more keenly on Rachel's underlying needs in order to promote better family relationships. But the question of how to respond to Rachel's immediate disciplinary needs inevitably demanded a response. "What am I supposed to do when Rachel storms out of the kitchen after slinging ketchup all over the place? I couldn't think of anything else to do except send her to her room and tell her she was grounded for the night."

Rachel's help was sought in answering her mother's question. The dilemma was presented to her. "Rachel, you put your mother between a rock and a hard place. She knew your stepfather shouldn't have been disrespectful to you, but she didn't think you should have thrown a temper tantrum to show how you felt."

"That's just it, she doesn't know how I feel! That's why I had to explode. If I didn't, nobody would know how bad I was feeling. They were yelling at me, so I yelled back just so they would know how I felt."

"So you made an overstatement of how you felt, hoping someone would see things your way."

"Right."

"Then it's safe to say that one of the things your mother could have done was to come to your room after you had a few minutes to cool off and let you talk about your anger." Rachel raised her eyebrows as if to say, "That would be nice, but I don't expect that to happen. If she came to my room it would be to lecture me."

I continued to think along with Rachel, "And it probably would be even nicer if your stepfather had come to your room to say he was sorry for his part in the blowup."

With that suggestion, Rachel groaned loudly. She could hardly imagine what I had suggested. "Him come to my room to apologize? Fat chance!"

"But just suppose he did," I persisted.

With her eyes glazed as if she was far away in thought, she said quietly, "That would be nice."

"But then your mom would probably still feel that you should stay in for the evening. She would think that if you went out with your friends she would have given in to your tantrum. You agree?"

Rachel looked at the ceiling and thought a moment. She shrugged her shoulders. "Probably."

"We could look at the situation positively, though. By staying in for the evening, your parents would have the opportunity to rebuild some bridges with you." Rachel smiled faintly. Inwardly she thought, *That would be nice, but I don't know if they would do it.*

To return to the mother's question about discipline, she was right to send Rachel to her room and keep her from going out that night. I should add, though, that the punishment chosen to correct an angry child's behavior is not nearly as important as the way the parent conducts herself before and after the punishment is rendered. Punishment typically has a limited effect on an angry young person. The family will only see improvement when the underlying communication from the teen is heard and responded to.

In the great Sermon on the Mount, Christ gave guidelines for living the Christian way of life. One of the beauties of Jesus' teachings is that the principles He offers for living can be applied to a wide range of roles we find ourselves in as adults. In Matthew 5:43–48,

Christ issues a law of love in which He tells us that love for those who oppose us overrides all other forms of influence. No one enjoys angry conflict that separates parent from child, but uncontrolled anger can do that to a family.

A teen who feels depressed and separated from her family needs the healing love of a parent that puts new focus on the relationship. One teen who had been through depression, but found renewed life through his family stated, "I used to be depressed because I couldn't do anything else with my anger. I couldn't get rid of it. But when things got better at home, I didn't need it anymore. It's feels good to get rid of all that emotion."

CHAPTER THIRTEEN

◆

I'm Not Sure Who I Am

ANGER CAN DISRUPT TEEN IDENTITY DEVELOPMENT

At a parent workshop I asked the participants, "How many of you would like to relive your adolescence? Please raise your hand." A few brave souls lifted a hand, but a majority of the adults simply snickered at the suggestion of voluntarily returning to their teen years. One man actually guffawed at the thought. When asked to give reasons for their resistant response the parents said:

- *Adolescence was an emotionally painful experience.*
- *I didn't like having to give in to my parents' authority.*
- *Not knowing how to relate to others was awkward and uncomfortable.*
- *I felt out of control during those years.*
- *I didn't know what was happening to my body as I went through puberty.*
- *I disliked being so dependent on others for financial support.*
- *I stayed confused most of the time and didn't really understand what life was all about.*
- *My emotions were so changeable; I had a hard time in relationships.*

A common statement made by teenagers is, "I can't wait until I'm an adult." Adults will say, "In a way the teen years were fun, but I'm glad I'm past that stage of life." These comments suggest that teens and adults alike understand the frustration associated with the teenage years. It is important that parents remember just how hard it was to be an adolescent. Teens need to know that we recognize their difficult position in life's cycle.

Just Who Am I Anyway?

As a psychologist people ask me many difficult questions. For all the tough issues I must face, though, none is more complex than the single question all teenagers must ask themselves: *Who am I?* This question has begged for an answer since the beginning of mankind. Adam and Eve grappled with questions of their identity as they tried, and failed, to make themselves equal to God. Since then, all men and women have gone through a similar search. That quest reaches its crescendo in adolescence.

Some teens do a pretty good job of looking at themselves honestly as they answer that question. Others, perhaps most, flounder as they struggle for acceptable answers. In reality, no teen can adequately solve this puzzle in a few short years. Adolescence only marks the beginning of our personal search for significance. But by establishing a firm foundation for identity development, the teen is more likely to be satisfied in knowing he is on the right road to reaching his potential.

It is typical for teenagers to define themselves by deciding what they do *not* want to be. I have heard teenagers often make these statements:

- *There's no way I'll be like my mother (father) when I'm an adult.*
- *I see so much prejudice and judgment in others; I'm not going to be that kind of person.*
- *I don't want to be just like everyone else. I'm my own person.*
- *You won't catch me being two-faced like most adults. I'll say exactly what I think!*

124

- *I just don't want to become a nobody.*
- *I don't want to take orders from others. I want to be the master of my own destiny.*

When teenagers define themselves by stating what they do not want to be, they often think it necessary to forcefully assert their feelings. Few parents want their children to grow up to be irresponsible, dependent adults. Parents desire for their children the same happiness their children want. Try to convince some teenagers that their parents' wishes match their own, though, and a stalemate will be the result.

CASE STUDY: *Mark Against the World*

Mark had just been suspended from school for three days. A rule at his high school forbade students from hanging posters of rock music stars in their hall lockers. Mark ignored the rule, claiming it was his right to put whatever he wished in his locker. In a confrontation with his principal he questioned the rule by asking, "What harm am I doing by putting a poster of a musician in my locker? How can that be so terrible?"

His principal, Mr. Warren, curtly responded, "It's terrible because those rock musicians fill teenagers' heads with nothing but filth. They encourage you to rebel. They tell you that if something feels good, you should just do it. They put down the idea that teenagers need to get along with others, especially adults. They play on your sexual urges by telling you to follow your sexual impulses. There, does that tell you why those posters are terrible?"

"No. It just tells me you're close-minded," Mark bluntly replied.

Irritated by Mark's impudence, Mr. Warren leaned forward toward the teenager and said, "Young man, you've got a long way to go before you know as much as you think you know. Why do you think that at age seventeen you have all the answers?" The disgusted principal felt a justified pleasure in punishing Mark with a school suspension.

Mark stood firmly opposed to Mr. Warren. He thought silently that he was glad to be more liberated in his thinking than the stodgy principal. Talking later with one of his friends he gave his opinion of the principal. "He's just like most adults. He pretends he's satisfied to live this dull, routine life. He just goes by the rule book. That's ridiculous! He doesn't know how to experiment with life. How can a man ever learn to appreciate life if he always goes by a dumb set of rules? That's not for me!"

Mr. Warren posed an interesting question when he asked Mark how he could be so certain of himself at just seventeen. Most adults who have encountered a confused, but unaware, teen have entertained the same thought. But it does little good to ask a teenager why he seems so convinced when he obviously lacks the experience and wisdom to answer life's difficult questions. The very fact that the teen latches so strongly to a "different" way of thinking gives evidence of his search for significance. I find those teenagers who are the most dogmatic about their rights, opinions, or beliefs to be the most confused. To defend themselves from their internal instability, they build walls around themselves to prop up their weak personal identity.

How Much Can a Parent Tolerate?

Teenagers like Mark are stating their need to "find" themselves. An angry teen's emotions can prevent him from accepting an adult's useful guidance. Mark would have benefited from the lessons about life his principal could teach him. He chose instead to follow his own uncertain ideals, which led him to damaging rebellion.

By understanding the teen's search for life's significance, parents can give that young person needed direction. But before giving such help, every parent needs to understand several facts of teen life:

- As the adolescent develops intellectually, he often questions the legitimacy of adults' authority. As youngsters, children more naturally accept an adult's leadership. Teenagers see themselves as capable of making their own judgments about life. The desire to test authority figures increases markedly during these years.
- Teenagers must choose between quietly accepting their parent's decisions or actively making their own choices. Both alternatives place the teen in a quandary since he may feel uncertain in either case.
- Teenagers must be allowed to make mistakes as they struggle to define themselves. A teen who does not occasionally stumble is at risk for making major mistakes later in life because decision-making skills are underdeveloped.
- Simultaneously, teens should not be encouraged to make mistakes that have grave consequences. A teenager who has made too many independent decisions is at risk of falling into a well so deep he cannot climb out.

As a parent understands these characteristics of adolescent life, it becomes easier to comprehend the wide mood swings and inconsistent behaviors of the teenager. The teen who lives with an understanding adult more willingly accepts parental help when he finds himself floundering. A balance between parental permissiveness and forcefulness must be delicately maintained. Respect for the teen's restless feelings tempered by well-timed intervention promotes emotional growth in the adolescent.

How a Teen Gathers Information about His Identity

A young person actually begins to develop his identity before he reaches adolescence. It is during adolescence that he tries to make sense of the feedback he has received in his short lifetime. Young children are like sponges—they soak up all the reactions and com-

ments other people offer. Their interpretation of what they have received forms their self-concept. Young children tend to assume that
adults are correct in the critique they offer. Teenagers, on the other
hand, actively question the opinions of their parents. The teen
searches to verify his worth by assuming various roles and behaviors.
Following are some examples of how a teen may test his self-concept.

- Fifteen-year-old Gina had been told throughout her childhood
  that she was creative. She wanted to believe her parents and
  teachers, but needed more proof. She submitted some poetry
  to her high school literary club and was pleasantly surprised
  that several of her works were printed in a school publication.
  Gina began to think that perhaps others were right when they
  referred to her as creative.

- Ricky had never been one to shy away from a fight. Now
  fifteen, it seemed he had tussled with every tough kid in his
  school. When his juvenile probation officer asked him what
  made him fight so frequently, he could only respond, "Hey,
  I've been fighting all my life. That's the kind of guy I am."

- Fifteen-year-old Jerry explained that as a child he had been
  neglected by his parents, sent to live with his grandmother,
  and separated from his two siblings. He explained to a girl
  who tried to befriend him, "You don't want to get close to me.
  Before long I'll probably be sent somewhere else to live. I don't
  count for much in my family."

It is little wonder that some teenagers struggle to define themselves. As the teen evaluates the feedback he receives from others
and attempts to match it with his childhood view of himself, the
pieces do not always fit neatly together. The chore of blending old
views with new personal discoveries takes time to successfully complete.

Adolescence Offers a Chance for Adjustments

During their child's adolescence parents often realize some parenting mistakes they made earlier in the child's life. There is good news in that discovery, though. By observing the way a teen tests his self-concept, parents can readily make adjustments to prevent the young person from several years of floundering. A teenage girl commented, "When I was a kid my parents used to spank me for everything wrong I did. When I got old enough, I started hitting back even though I knew it was wrong. When things got out of hand, my mother broke down and asked me what she could do to keep me from being so hateful to her. I told her I was tired of being treated like a nobody, being hit and yelled at all the time. You know what? She quit doing all those things to me. For the first time in my life, I felt like my mother tried to understand me. We get along a lot better now."

The adjustment this mother made to her daughter's anger allowed the girl to be more responsible to herself and others. A teenager's identity development is strongly influenced by the relationships he has with his parents. Parents who respond with understanding to the teen's emotional needs can become his ally rather than his foe. I'd like to offer some guidelines to help the teenager answer that difficult question, *Who am I?*

- *Show patience in the face of your teen's impulses.* Teenagers are notorious for making rash decisions without thinking of the potential consequences of their choices. It is tempting to quickly correct obvious teen mistakes. However, teenagers will often become stubborn when they hear premature advice. Trying to force "truth" on an uncertain youth can hurt family relations. Said one young man, "I hate it that my father thinks he's right all the time. Maybe he is, but it makes me mad that he tries to force his way on me." When parents show patient understanding, teens are more likely to solicit their input.

- *Use your powers of positive persuasion.* Earlier I referred to the young child as a "sponge" that absorbs feedback from others into his self-concept. Although teenagers often look more to their peers for approval than family members, the impact of well-placed positive reinforcement from parents is still powerful. After his mother complimented him for the way he kept his cool when a friend had betrayed him, a teenager asked, "Mom, do you think I could have handled things any differently?" He was open to the suggestions of a parent he perceived to be on his side.

- *Constantly update your inventory of the expectations you have for your teen.* As a parent thought back on his daughter's decision to quit the school basketball team, he commented, "At first I was disappointed in her decision, but as I thought about it, I realized I wanted her to satisfy *my* desires, not hers. She wanted to become more involved in photography. She's perfectly happy in her new activity. Why shouldn't I be happy that she's happy?" When teenagers feel pressure to live up to parents' ideals, they may angrily resist. We should make sure we do not expect for our children more than they want or need.

- *Demonstrate to your teen that adult life is still fun.* Some teenagers assume that after their twentieth birthday has past, life loses its zip. Teens want to see that adult life has something positive to offer. As much as we hate to admit it, adults sometimes do little to demonstrate that there can be happiness beyond adolescence. A sixteen-year-old girl who had contemplated suicide pointed at the despair she saw in her parents' life. "I hate being a teenager and can't wait to be older. But when I see how my parents fight and stay miserable all the time, it makes me think that being an adult stinks. Life doesn't get any better, so why keep going?"

- *Talk openly about spiritual matters.* For the first time in their life, teenagers can comprehend many of the spiritual truths they may have been taught in their earlier years. One young man related, "I have been going to church all my life. I knew what the Bible said about God, but to tell you the truth, I didn't understand it. I don't want to scare anybody with all my questions, but I really want to know why people believe the things they believe." It's exciting to know your teenager is seeking answers to spiritual problems. A teen who sees openness and composure in his parents will lean on them to settle his uncertainty. Parents who try to force answers on a doubting teen will push him away in anger.

Teenagers may balk, even rebel, if parents try to force answers to difficult questions about identity. However, a parental stance that helps the teenager come to *his own* conclusions about his values, morals, and spirituality is almost certain to be welcomed. Patient understanding serves as a stabilizer to a wavering teenager.

Section Three

HOW TEENAGE ANGER
GETS OUT OF CONTROL

◆

CHAPTER FOURTEEN

Who Can the Teen Depend On?

TEEN DEPENDENCE ON PARENTS CAN FUEL ANGER

I don't need anyone and I for sure don't need my parents!" Lonnie adamantly believed that he was ready to tackle the world.

"How's that?" I asked.

"Look, I'm sixteen years old. I have a job that pays me $4.50 an hour. I've got my own car. I have my friends. I'm doing all right in school. People like me. What else do I need? I don't need my parents. I don't need anything from them at all. They can just butt out of my life."

"So what is it you want from your parents?"

"I want them to let me decide what I'm going to do about school. They keep telling me which college they want me to go to. Who knows, I may not go to college! They try to pick my friends. Well, they can just forget that. I want to hang around the people I like, not the people they think are good for me. And they try to tell me where I should go when I go out at night and when I need to be home. How can they know what's best for me? They should let me decide what I'm going to do. I'm a big boy!" Lonnie's voice dripped with sarcasm.

"So you depend on your parents a lot."

"Huh?" Lonnie was confused, to say nothing of irritated. He had just detailed reasons he did *not* need his parents, yet here I was claiming it was obvious he was dependent on them.

"What I mean is that for you to live the kind of life you want, you depend on your parents to stay out of your way."

"Yeah, but they won't."

"So you try to force them to butt out."

"Yeah, but it doesn't work. They won't leave me alone."

"I guess the harder you try to force your parents to give you independence, the more convinced they become that they need to tighten up on you. It's a vicious cycle. How do you get out of it?"

Lonnie's irritation was gone. He was now interested in knowing what could be done to free him from the tight reins of his parents. "I can't. Nothing seems to work. Every time I try to get them off my back, they get stricter. I'll yell at them and tell them to leave me alone, but they won't. I don't think they believe me that I can be my own person. Are you saying there's something I can do to get them to quit bugging me?"

"You haven't done a good enough job convincing them."

"You mean I need to rebel?" Lonnie was more than willing to be even more defiant if that's what it took to get what he wanted.

"You've already tried that and it didn't work. That's the problem. By rebelling, you haven't convinced your parents that you're the responsible person you claim to be."

"Brother! So what am I supposed to do, be a sweet little angel? That's exactly what they want, but I don't want to give in to them." Lonnie envisioned himself holding out a white flag of surrender to his parents. The thought of losing a hard-fought power struggle did not appeal to him.

"Let's talk about what you may be doing with anger that's getting in your way." From there, Lonnie talked about how he was hurting his chances of being independent from his parents.

Whether the Teen Likes It or Not, He's Dependent

Lonnie's comments are typical of many teenagers. Many teens are convinced they do not need their parents to steer them through life's curves. One way or another, teens are dependent on their parents, even if it is merely to stay out of their way.

A simple fact of adolescent life is that no teenager is completely independent of others, especially his parents. Though the teenager may want to see a wider gap between himself and his parents, he still needs their guidance. A task of the parent is to judge just how much latitude to give the mistake-prone teenager. In Lonnie's case, his rebellion convinced his mother and father to exercise stronger parental authority than he wanted. In actuality, Lonnie probably could have handled more of the freedom he desired. Responding to his anger correctly could relieve him from the suffocation he felt while also soothing his parents' natural desire to keep him from unnecessary harm.

Let's look at two scenarios involving an independent-minded teenager and how parents may interpret this behavior. The underlying teen communication will be uncovered. I will then examine how some parental responses may provoke further anger rather than reduce it. Effective alternatives will then be offered.

PROBLEM SITUATION #1: By late afternoon Andrea had failed to wash a load of laundry as her mother had requested that morning before leaving for work. When Mother walked into the house, she discovered her daughter lying on the couch watching TV. She asked Andrea why the clothes had not been washed. Andrea offered a limp excuse as she turned the TV volume up louder so her mother's voice would not drown out the set. She showed no signs of getting up to start the load of laundry.

PARENT'S INTERPRETATION: "My daughter is lazy. If I don't teach her to follow simple instructions, she may not learn to be responsible to others."

TEEN'S INTENDED COMMUNICATION: "I'll wash the load of clothes, but I'd like to do it when it's convenient for me. I know how to take care of my own responsibilities."

HARMFUL PARENT REACTION: Stomping to the TV set, Mother turns it off. She wheels around and looks at her daughter, shouting, "I'm not about to let you lie there on that couch acting lazy while I'm at work trying to earn enough money to buy what this family needs. Now get in there right now and wash those clothes like I told you to do this morning!"

Andrea argues with her mother, stating she will do it once her show is over. After fifteen long minutes of arguing, Andrea trudges to the dirty clothes hamper, gets out about half a load of clothes, and washes them. She intentionally fails to put enough detergent in the washing machine, hoping to leave stains on some of the laundry items.

HELPFUL PARENT REACTION: Mother is upset that Andrea has not washed a load of clothes as was requested. She realizes, though, that since she was not home all day, she had limited control in seeing to it that Andrea followed through with her chore. She tells Andrea she wants the clothes washed right away. Andrea promises to put a load in the washer in ten minutes after her show is over. Once the allotted time has passed, Mother returns to the living room to make sure Andrea follows through on her responsibility. She says little to Andrea, but thanks her as the girl crawls off the couch to do her job. Andrea unenthusiastically, but dutifully, carries out the task.

COMMENT: Andrea wanted to decide when she would fulfill the job she was asked to do—a reasonable request. Her mother's interpretation that Andrea needed to learn a lesson in responsibility was correct. Andrea's procrastination indicated she was not being as responsible as her mother felt she should be. To yell at her and accuse her of laziness, though, only created resentment in Andrea. At that point, focus shifted to the struggle for control between the mother and daughter.

In the second scenario—when the mother imposed reasonable boundaries in a calmer fashion—the teen responded more favorably. Mother's aim of teaching her daughter to become independent was more likely realized. Although Andrea did not like the boundaries her mother placed around her, the second response created less anger, and its accompanying resentment, than the first

PROBLEM SITUATION #2: Larry was not paying attention as he backed his dad's car out of the driveway. He rammed it into a corner of the house, breaking one of the rear brake lights. He knew that if he immediately told his father of his accident, he would not be allowed to take the car out that night. He opted to wait until later in the evening to inform his dad of the mishap. When he gave his father the bad news, Dad was understandably dismayed to hear of his son's error.

PARENT'S INTERPRETATION: "My son made a foolish mistake and needs to accept the consequences of his error. He has also been deceitful by waiting to tell me just to avoid having to 'face the music.'"

TEEN'S INTENDED COMMUNICATION: "I know I'll have to face up to my mistake eventually. I'm afraid if I tell my dad right away what I've done, though, he'll keep me from my social activities. I'll tell him later when it's more convenient for me. That way, I can go where I want tonight, but still be honest with Dad about my mistake."

HARMFUL PARENT REACTION: After Larry comes home he informs his dad that he accidentally backed the car into the corner of the house, breaking the rear lights. His Dad becomes angry and confronts the youth. "You mean you did this as you were backing out of the driveway three hours ago? You've been driving around without your brake lights working? I can't believe you would do something that foolish! Don't you realize you could get a ticket? I can't depend on you to do the right thing. Now do you see why I don't trust you to do everything you ask to do? You can forget about driving my car anytime soon. And you had better find some way to come up with enough money to pay for the damage!"

Larry stands quietly as his father berates him, thinking, *That's exactly why I don't tell him any more than I have to. I hate listening to his temper outbursts.*

HELPFUL PARENT REACTION: Upon hearing Larry's explanation of what he had done to the car as he backed out of the driveway, Dad feels upset, but keeps his composure. "It's not easy for you to have to tell me that you've broken out the rear lights in my car." The look on Larry's face validates that obvious fact. "I suppose there's a reason you waited until you got home to tell me rather than inform me right after it happened?"

Larry explains to his father, "I knew you would be mad and probably wouldn't let me take the car out."

Dad honestly states, "Yeah, I'm upset." Not belaboring his anger, though, he adds, "Now we need to figure out what to do about this problem. It's not smart to drive a car without the brake lights working." He waited for suggestions from Larry.

Seeing that the burden of responsibility had been placed on his shoulders, Larry thought aloud, "I guess we need to get it fixed as soon as we can. Do I have to pay for it?" Dad nodded quietly, giving Larry the response he expected. Though he did not announce it at the time, Dad quietly resolved to be more stringent with Larry's driving privileges in the near future.

COMMENT: Larry knew he had made a mistake and would have to pay for it. His dilemma was to decide how he would break the news to his father. He did not want to face immediate discipline and chose to wait until later to inform his dad of his mistake. In his way of thinking, he could just as easily be held accountable for his mistake after an enjoyable evening. As self-centered as that thought might be, it is understandable.

Dad's first reaction only reinforced Larry's distaste for his father's authority. Dad's angry outburst actually encouraged the teen to continue in his deceit. By responding angrily, he increased the likelihood that Larry would retaliate. Larry's deceit was a passive form of exerting control over his father.

The second alternative shows Dad controlling his upset emotions. He acknowledges his son's fear, but does not neglect his own frustration and disappointment. Dad knows, however, that to dwell on his anger will only heighten the resentment in Larry. He chooses not to emotionally pound his son. He lets his emotions be known, but then deals with the problem and lays it to rest. Larry is more likely to think, *I know my Dad is not happy with me, but he treated me with dignity. I can be honest with a man who offers me that kind of respect.*

Lead Your Teen toward Independence

Perhaps one of the greatest sources of parental confusion lies in knowing when to let go and let a teenager make his own choices. An exasperated mother asked, "What should I do to let my son be more independent? He seems bound and determined that he's not going to listen to me, so I might as well give in and let him be his own person. But if I'm going to let him go, I want to do it the right way."

Although this mother's request grew out of frustration, she was taking an important step. She was right in recognizing that her son was going to be independent, regardless of how much she intervened. Even if he could not behave independently, he would think independently. She was also correct in realizing there is both a right way and a wrong way to guide a teen toward independence.

We may mistakenly think that by giving our teenagers independence, we automatically throw away our influence in their lives. Actually, by pushing personal freedom on a teenager correctly, the parent places herself in a position to be *increasingly* influential.

CASE STUDY: *Gwen and Her Grades*

Gwen was trying to decide which courses to take in her upcoming sophomore year in high school. She had been an honor student, but was tired of the constant study her advanced classes required. After talking to her school counselor, Gwen decided to drop two of her most difficult classes in favor of easier classes in the fall semester.

The teen had mixed feelings about telling her mother about her decision. She was afraid of being accused of taking the easy route to a high school education. On the other hand, she reasoned the extra time could be used to pursue other extracurricular activities she had not previously had time to enjoy. To the girl's surprise and delight, Mother passively accepted the teen's decision to change her schedule. Mother and daughter agreed they would evaluate the success of Gwen's experiment at the end of one semester.

The following months saw Gwen stagnate. Instead of becoming more involved in other activities, she became less active. Her grades in the easier classes were lower than those she had made in the advanced classes.

One evening Mother approached Gwen to talk about her school status. "I think it's time we talk about your experiment this semester. How do you think it's going?"

Gwen laughed uncomfortably. "Things haven't gone like I had planned. I guess it's all right, though. I'm doing fine in school."

"What kind of grades do you think you'll make this six weeks?"

"Pretty good."

"It seems you did better last year when you were taking harder classes. That's odd. What do you figure Dad and I think about your status right now?"

"Are you mad?"

"No, we're not mad. We do think you haven't been as productive as you're capable of being."

"What are you going to make me do?"

"What are your options?"

"Well, I could either stay in the same classes, or ask Mr. Talley to put me back in the honors classes."

"But you'd be behind if you went back into the honors classes."

"I could catch up. I've already talked with Mrs. Lewis about getting into her English class, and she says she can make sure I don't fall too far behind the rest of the class."

"You mean you've already been talking to your teachers about getting back into your old schedule?"

Gwen chuckled. "Yes. I've heard Mrs. Lewis's English class really helps you get ready for your college board exams, and I need all the help I can get. I think I'm slipping in my class ranking. I need to do something to get my grades up."

"It's important to do well in school. You've got a lot riding on your high school grades." Mother refrained from making up her daughter's mind for her. Her intent was to move with Gwen through her entire range of thoughts about school.

At the end of their conversation, Gwen told her mom, "I'm going to talk to Mr. Talley tomorrow during my lunch break." Mom made no outward evaluation of her judgment, but was pleased to see Gwen think objectively about her own educational needs.

As a group of parents heard this story, one parent remarked, "That makes a nice illustration, but I know if I gave my son the latitude to make his own decisions, they would all be wrong." Several other parents shook their heads indicating that they could identify with this man's concern.

Let's look at the dynamics at work between Gwen and her mother to understand why this mother acted as she did. The guidelines she followed can be applied to teenagers who are not as level-headed as Gwen:

- Mother was initially unexcited about Gwen's desire to take an easier class schedule. Yet, she recognized that she should not force her own judgment on the teen. She knew Gwen was starving to be independent. She also knew that by preventing Gwen's independence, she was inviting hostility. She concluded that if she were to have an effective influence over her daughter on school matters it was important to allow Gwen a choice in this matter.

- Gwen's mother did not let her make a decision that would have catastrophic results. The girl's plan to become more involved in other activities potentially offered her the chance to receive a different—yet adequate—education.

- As Mother and Gwen agreed to Gwen's plan of action, they also agreed to reassess its effectiveness at a later date. This strategy ensured that Gwen would be held accountable for the results of her choice.

- Later, when Gwen and her mother met to evaluate the teen's change of schedule, Mother refrained from pointing out the girl's failures. She was not interested in "winning" an argument. She knew Gwen was fully aware of her feelings, making it unnecessary to enumerate them. Instead, she allowed Gwen to assess her current progress in school. Mother knew that by allowing the problem to remain with Gwen, the teen was more likely to make a wise choice, which she did.

When teenagers are not likely to act as responsibly as Gwen did, the parent will need to provide a more narrow range of choices. A teenager with a poor track record might be given the choice between two classes that are acceptable both to the teen and the parent. Evaluations of the teen's performance would be needed more frequently so adjustments could be quickly made to keep the youth moving toward responsible independence.

Even though teenagers require differing degrees of accountability, all need to be shown respect for their choices. The teenager needs to learn to make choices that are his, not ours. Within acceptable boundaries, teens need to feel self-sufficient. That is a powerful feeling to a teenager.

Ironically, as teenagers are allowed to make choices, they will frequently seek parental input. They do not want to fail in life. If the teen is convinced his parents think he can succeed, he will seek their advice. Anger can then be removed from the fight for independence.

◆

CHAPTER FIFTEEN

Does Anybody Know I'm Here?

ANGRY TEENS OFTEN FEEL LONELY

Oasne of the most troubling developments of our generation has been the swell of teenage crime and its related rebellion. We tend to think of teen crime as an inner city problem. Yet it reaches all corners of our society. Many parents now will not allow their children to participate in previously safe activities. A mother refuses to let her children walk a few blocks to school for fear that they will become front page news at the hands of a deranged abductor. A dad insists that his teenage children tell him where they will be at all times. He does not mean to intrude in the lives of his children. He simply wants to be spared the horror of not knowing if his children have become crime victims.

Many criminal offenders are teenagers. I have known many teens whose violence is their exaggerated way of making a statement to society. Even though each has a personal story of how he became an angry youth, these teens are communicating, *I'm angry and I want the whole world to know!* As harsh as this statement is, there is almost always a second message attached: *I'm lonely. Does anybody know I'm here?*

Loneliness is a terrible feeling. A lonely teenager feels so ignored that he seriously questions his personal value. Aggressive, lonely teenagers often make remarks such as:

- *Why bother talking to adults. They won't listen anyway.*
- *It's a chore to get through the day. I don't care about my life.*
- *I'd rather be by myself. Other people just ignore me. I can't stand the rejection.*
- *I don't feel close to anyone—not even my family.*
- *I get into trouble when I feel the most isolated.*
- *I don't even bother to tell others how I really feel. They wouldn't understand. It's easier to try to ignore my feelings.*
- *I don't do anything right. If you don't believe me, come to my house and watch how much I'm criticized.*

Can you sense the anger in these statements? Other intense emotions are beneath feelings of loneliness. These emotions often go unnoticed by others, but this does make them less intense. They are ignored because most of us have trouble "reading" the telltale signs of loneliness. We may mistakenly assume that lonely teenagers want to be left alone. We think, *If he wanted companionship, surely he would seek it out.* In actuality, the teen often thinks, *I'd like to feel close to others, but I don't know how to initiate meaningful relationships.* Their aggressive behavior is evidence of the frustration they feel.

CASE STUDY: *Tony's Loneliness Leads to Vandalism*

Fifteen-year-old Tony was out late at night doing nothing in particular. He had spent some time at the house of an acquaintance who had been host to an "all-comers" beer party. Tony hung around the boy's house a while and drank his fair share of alcohol. When several other boys suggested he come along with them as they drove around, he joined in. All the boys had been drinking and wanted an outlet for their pent-up emotions.

"Let's go to Riverbend and bash a few mailboxes," suggested one of the guys. The other boys in the car quickly endorsed the scheme. None of them had an affinity for the people who lived in that wealthy area of town. Tony was sitting in the back seat of the car, next to a window. As the rowdy crew rode down a neighborhood street, one of his companions handed him a baseball bat and goaded him to smash a mailbox as the driver zoomed by a house.

Tony mindlessly complied, but the force of the blow caused him to drop the bat as he made contact with the mailbox. The other boys howled with laughter, ridiculing Tony for being so graceless. The car screeched to a halt so Tony could retrieve his bat. As Tony got out of the car, one of the other boys encouraged the driver to leave him. "He's a geek anyway." Unconcerned for Tony's welfare, the carload of teenagers left him standing alone in the neighborhood street screaming and cursing at their behavior.

The boy made such commotion that the police were called. Within minutes, Tony was confronted by two policemen who had a seemingly endless list of questions about his disregard for the law.

An angry, defensive Tony showed up in my office two days after this incident occurred. He virtually refused to look at me and only mumbled when he spoke. Eventually the conversation focused on his family. "I hate them" was his first comment about his mother and father.

"Those are strong words," I replied.

Tony shot back accusingly, "They don't even care that I'm in trouble. They say that maybe it will teach me a lesson. I think they want me to get into big trouble. Some parents, huh? What do you think of a mother and father who don't even care if their son is in trouble with the law? You'd think they'd want to help me out, but they won't. Do you know what my dad told the police when they called him the night they picked me up? He said to just leave me in jail until the next morning. He didn't want to get out of bed. Like I said, they don't care." Tony was so upset, he was breathing heavily.

"You say they hope you've been taught a lesson. You probably have learned something from this experience. What was it?"

Tony burst out, "I've learned that I don't matter much! They say I'm a loser and maybe I am."

149

"I doubt that's the lesson they want you to learn."

Tony laughed cynically. "They want me to learn to act right. They want me to be a sweet little boy who doesn't do anything to ruin the family's reputation. They want me to be who *they* want me to be. It's like my feelings don't even exist."

"But it's obvious your feelings do exist."

"Yeah, but nobody knows what they are." Tony still gazed downward.

"You mean you keep your feelings to yourself most of the time?"

Tony was quiet now. His voice softened. Politely, he said, "Yes, sir." The boy hung his head, trying to hold back his hurt feelings. Failing to squash his emotions, though, tears began to trickle down his cheeks. Wiping his eyes he said, "I hate to cry."

Seeing that Tony hated his loneliness more than he hated to cry, I commented, "When you cry, a lot of bitter feelings come with the tears, don't they?" Tony simply nodded his head. His entire body was weary with desperation.

That conversation with Tony raised many questions, but one stood higher than the others. *What had happened in Tony's life to convince him he was inferior to others?* Why did he refer to himself as a "loser"? His bad experience at the hands of his "friends" had simply become, in his mind, part of a backlog of evidence of his worthlessness. To prove his lowly position, he pointed out that even his mother and father did not care for him. All of Tony's behavior demonstrated his deep feeling of isolation from others, including his family. His impulsive escapade with his peers highlighted how low he would sink in order to gain acceptance from others.

Loneliness Pushes Feelings Underground

Tony had difficulty attaching words to his feelings. In their place, he used reckless behavior to speak for him. Lonely teenagers are usually poor verbal communicators of their feelings. They have a hard time expressing what is inside them. Yet, a rule of communication is that feelings always get expressed. Children who cannot verbalize their emotions find other, often aggressive, ways to release them. After being so tightly held, their emotions ache for release.

Ways a lonely teenager may cling to his emotions include:

- *Sleep disturbances* The teen may have difficulty falling asleep or may sleep excessively. Night terrors or nightmares may represent the frightening impact of the young person's anxiety.
- *Physical complaints* Withheld emotions can surface in a teenager's body. Headaches, stomachaches, chronic fatigue, or other ailments may highlight the young person's need for care from others.
- *Immature behavior* Some lonely teens will act as if they are much younger than they are. They may even talk like a young child at times. This behavior symbolizes a wish for the kind of nurturing care that is given to small children.
- *Calloused aggression* Aggression that victimizes others reveals the intensity of unspoken emotions. To protect himself against emotional hurt, the young person builds a wall of contempt around himself.
- *Withdrawal and depression* Lonely teens may give up their hope that life will get better. They may feel that emotional withdrawal is the only safe way to avoid being hurt further by life. They may even entertain suicidal thoughts.

Ways a lonely teen may go to opposite extremes and let emotions go without inhibition include:

- *Destructiveness* Physical destruction of property may release the rage inside the adolescent. It may also provide a picture of how the teen would like to hurt others or even himself.
- *Irritating others* The lonely teenager is exasperated that his emotional needs are being ignored. He may annoy others to both

draw attention to his needs and show others how it feels to be isolated.

- *Victimizing others* To hurt others offers the teen an opportunity to gain revenge for his own emotional discomfort. In some extreme cases, teens victimize others to express self-destructive thoughts.
- *Sexual acting out* Some lonely teens see sexual activity as a way to gain the affection they feel they have missed. Some use sex as a way to control others. In still other cases, sexual promiscuity provides a way for the teen to punish parents by disregarding one of their most sacred rules.

Anger Sends the Lonely Teen the Wrong Message

When a teenager has no one to turn to for direction, he makes the best judgments he can. Sometimes he stuffs his feelings with the faint hope that they will evaporate. At other times he lets them rip, not caring who knows how desperate he feels. If the teen is honest with himself, he will admit to feeling hopelessly lost.

Tony was an isolated teen who felt he could not turn to his parents for help. He temporarily trusted his peer group who convinced him he could find happiness by abandoning the rules of society. When they left him alone at night in the middle of the street, he quickly learned he could not count on them to offer him what he was looking for in life.

During a conversation with Tony I asked him, "Tony, what do you think is going to happen to you in life?"

As if the thought of the future had not entered his mind, Tony drew a blank look on his face as he said, "I don't know. I never thought that far ahead."

"How far ahead do you think?" he was asked.

"I don't," he said bluntly.

Trying to understand Tony's thought process, I replied, "If you thought too far ahead, you probably wouldn't like what you saw. It must be easier to just ignore the future. Maybe if you ignore it, your worst dreams won't come true." The youth nodded his head. That statement summarized his listless attitude about the future. He ignored it because thinking about it hurt too much.

Tony's anger toward life had encouraged him to draw at least one conclusion: *Ignore as much as you can about life. It doesn't have much to offer you anyway. Ignore your parents, your friends, your teachers, and anyone else who says they can help you make a brighter future. They can't.* That message was not helpful to Tony. Of all people, he needed a sense of hope about the future. He needed to be told, "Tony, life has more to offer you than your past would suggest. Have faith that your life will get better." You can imagine the reaction Tony, or any other discouraged youth, would have to that statement. It probably would not be positive, but it is a message he needs to hear.

Lonely Teenagers Need a Reason to Trust

The hurt of aimless, angry, aggressive teenagers like Tony bruises the entire family. Parents feel frustrated when the teenager refuses to accept the wisdom the adults would like to share. As exasperated as parents feel over their child's behavior, it is even more frustrating to be a teenager who wants to believe there is hope in the world, but has no reason to believe. A lonely teenager *wants* to be told over and over again that there is reason for him to have faith in life. He has been hurt in relationships so frequently, though, that reasons to trust are hard to find.

The anger of loneliness can be broken. But it takes leadership on the part of the parent to push away this damaging emotion. Healing in an angry, lonely youth is fostered by parents who try the following.

- Look at your parental role as an opportunity to provide leadership to your teenager. Do not wait for him to surrender in defeat before you do all you can to improve family relations.

Make the first move to reestablish yourself as a significant person in your child's life.

- Eliminate certain negative phrases from your communication with your teenager. Phrases begining with "You never . . ." or "You always . . ." or "You should . . ." or "I won't . . ." frequently send messages of judgment to the teen. A teen who feels judged will not want to express his feelings honestly.

- Recognize the value of time spent with your teenager. Spending time with a young person does not have to cost money. You do not have to talk about anything in particular with the teen. Committing to make your teen an important part of your day erases his belief that he is insignificant. He may feel awkward initially, but will appreciate your time.

- Let your teenager express his feelings. When teens first verbalize their emotions, their tendency is to let go of them with force. An adult's tendency is to recoil with a counter force. Quietly listening before reacting can often "take the wind out of his sails" and make him more willing to respond to your leadership. A teen who has talked out his feelings does not have that urge to blast others with his anger.

- Be honest in expressing your own emotions, but do not use them to hurt. Parents hurt teenagers with their words when they fail to exhibit emotional control. Honest emotional expression requires the parent to use good timing in showing feelings. A teen may hear the right message, but if he hears it at the wrong time, its effect can be the opposite of its intent.

- Give your teenager time to heal. Anger damages teenagers in many ways. When repairing any kind of personal damage, time is one of the family's most important allies. Teens often welcome positive changes in the home, but are usually leery that those changes will not last. An uncertain teen will challenge the seriousness of his parents by testing limits. This behavior is the teen's way of asking, "Do you mean it when you promise to treat me differently, or will we return to the same old way of relating to each other?"

Lonely teenagers are prone to think they are the only ones who feel the way they do. They may join forces with other groping teens hoping to find company in their isolation. Even though they may run in groups, their relationships are typically empty. Their anger encourages them to keep a safe distance from others, not because they want to remain lonely, but because they are fearful. Understanding the emotions of the teenager helps the parent give the youth the direction he needs. Parents may love their angry teenager unconditionally, but that love must be communicated to the teen for him to use it to his advantage.

CHAPTER SIXTEEN

◆

Everything's Going My Way

A SPOILED TEEN IS AN ANGRY TEEN

S ure I'm spoiled. I don't mind admitting it. It's not my fault my parents give me everything. Hey, if they're going to be that way, I'm sure not going to tell them to change. Why would I? I'm not dumb, you know."

Making that statement was a pretty sixteen-year-old girl, Pamela, whose parents were increasingly unsettled about her disregard for their household rules. She was a likable girl, but had a, well, sassy air about her.

Leaning forward in her chair as if she were about to tell a secret, Pamela continued, "Do you know what happened yesterday? I came in late from school and my mother demanded to know where I had been. I had been at my boyfriend's house—don't tell my parents—but I told her I was at a friend's house looking at some jewelry her mother sells. I had to make the story sound believable, so I went into all this detail about wanting to buy a certain bracelet. Instead of getting mad at me for being late, my mother asked me how much the bracelet costs. I told her twenty-five dollars. Then she went to her purse and got out twenty-five dollars and gave it to me! She told me it could be an early birthday present."

"Suppose she wants to see the bracelet she thought she was paying for?"

"I can guarantee you she's already forgotten about that bracelet. All I know is I got twenty-five dollars for coming home late and telling my mother some cock and bull story. Now do you see why

I'm not about to tell my parents I'm spoiled? I figure that what they don't know won't hurt them—and it may help me!" Pamela laughed at her own shrewdness.

Nice Kids Can Be Easily Spoiled

Pamela's parents, Mr. and Mrs. Penders, were confused by their daughter's behavior. "We're not exactly sure where we went wrong," explained Mr. Penders, searching to understand his daughter. "We *do* spoil her, but not so bad that she should treat us like we're her servants. I might as well tell you that I'm probably more guilty of spoiling her than Patsy. We both give her too much, but I *know* I overdo it. My schedule at work is pretty hectic. Sometimes I'll have several weeks straight of twelve hour days. That doesn't give me much time with the kids, so I tend to buy them whatever I can to make up for the time I'm away from home. I can justify the expense because I get overtime pay for working the extra hours. It's just that Pamela seems to want more than everyone else."

"But she hasn't always been that way, has she?" I asked, trying to find the origin of the teen's disobedient behavior.

Mrs. Penders spoke up. "Oh no! It's only in the last two years that Pamela has turned into this monster. We used to think she appreciated whatever we did for her, so we did more for her whenever we could. We just wanted to make life easier for her than we had it. There's nothing wrong with that. She's just gotten to where she expects too much from us." She sighed as she finished her comment, her body so full of emotions she could hardly contain them.

Many young people lull their parents into spoiling them. A pattern is often followed in families of spoiled adolescents:

- Early in their childhood, the young person seems grateful to her parents for the extra pleasures provided to her.
- As time passes, those things that were once "perks" become expected fare. No longer satisfied with small favors or material

158

gifts, the young person expects, even demands, to be treated like royalty.

- Not wanting to face the inevitable fuss that will follow if extra privileges or material items are withheld, the parent gives in to the young person's demands. It is hoped the gesture will be appreciated.
- Instead of appreciating all that has been done for her, the teen devalues both the "extras" of life and those who are so quick to give in to her demands.
- The demands of the teen become increasingly intolerable. A long series of power struggles ensues with the parents trying to regain their authority over the teen and the teen fighting to keep from losing her privileged status.

When parents grant special favors to their children, they certainly do not intend to create an ungrateful teenager. Every parent enjoys seeing the gleam in the eye of a child who has been surprised with a gift or favor. Not only does the experience lift the child's spirits, it boosts the parent as well. Anger may unexpectedly wind its way into a young person's heart when giving is not balanced with an expectation that he also needs to give. When demands are made of him, a teenager may be easily offended because he has not learned to look beyond his needs to other people.

A Spoiled Teen Dislikes the Word No

A spoiled teen's least favorite word is *no*. It is amazing that the simplest of words can dominate family relationships. A spoiled teenager comes to view the word "no" as a signal to merely try harder to get his way. The ensuing fight for control discourages the young person from looking beyond himself to the needs of others.

I asked Pamela what she did when her parents said no to her requests. She bluntly said, "Oh, I ignore them when they tell me that. I know I can get them to change their mind."

"You sound confident that you know exactly what to do."

Pamela *was* confident and showed it as she willingly laid out her modus operandi. "You see, I know my parents don't want to fight with me. They hate that because I can make life pretty miserable for them. When they tell me I can't do something or have what I really want, I fight." Pamela wore a smile that teemed with cocky confidence.

"You mean if you can get them into a fight, you're confident you can get them to give in?"

"A lot of the time."

"Enough to make it worth your effort to give it a try."

"Right."

"But what about those times your parents stick to their guns and refuse to give in? How do you handle those times?"

"I know I can't have everything. Don't get me wrong. I'm not a total jerk. But if my parents don't give in on something I think is real important, I'm going to make sure they pay for it."

"By doing what?"

"I'm going to make sure they feel just as bad as I do. If I'm mad, they're going to be mad, too."

"Even though you and your parents are mad about different things, you're even because nobody is happy." Pamela bobbed her head up and down.

"That seems like a high price for the family to pay just because one person is mad," I commented. Pamela shrugged her shoulders indifferently. Her gesture suggested she felt justified for acting as she did when she heard the word "no."

It was evident that Pamela had studied her parents for years in order to learn what worked to manipulate them in her favor. She was so certain of her ability to successfully maneuver the family, she did not mind sharing her secrets with others. It was as if she was saying, *This is how I use my anger to get my way. Try to stop me if you think you can.*

I asked Pamela to step back in time to uncover how she changed from a conforming child to a rebellious teenager. "Pamela, your parents say you weren't always so hard to handle. They say that over the last couple of years things have gotten worse at home. What happened?"

Pamela thought for a moment. "I don't know. I don't think *I* did anything to make things go downhill." She honestly believed her behavior was justified.

"You mean you were only reacting to the way your parents were handling you?"

"Well, yeah. I guess so. They're the parents. I was just doing what they let me do."

With those few words Pamela had revealed an important clue about how she turned from compliance to rebellion. She stated, "I was just doing what they let me do." "What they let her do" set the emotional tempo of the home. Over the course of time, Pamela had absorbed many behavior-shaping messages from her parents. They included:

- *We want you to be happy, so we will do whatever we can to ensure your happiness.*
- *Our satisfaction depends on you. If you are satisfied, we are satisfied.*
- *If you are unhappy, we will try to rid you of your discomfort.*
- *We are uncertain where the boundaries of our authority are in the home.*
- *Our emotions can be manipulated.*

Pamela took advantage of the chance to place herself in the position of control of the family. She did not like the word "no," so she did what she could to purge it from her parents' vocabulary. Recognizing her parents' inconsistency and their susceptibility to emotional manipulation, she gradually gained power. Her greatest problem was that she did not see a need for discipline in her life. Feeling she could manipulate her way through life just as she had weaved through the power structure of the home, she was ripe for disappointment.

A Spoiled Teen Has Unrealistic Expectations of the World

Problems are inevitable when a teenager expects the world to treat them just as their families have. Spoiled teens tend to assume that the others can be just as easily maneuvered as family members. Experience has taught them that rules apply to others, but not to them. Having been the exception to the rule, the teen will assume entitlement from society.

Mr. and Mrs. Penders were embarrassed by their daughter's blunders at school and in the community. Mrs. Penders rolled her eyes as she talked of Pamela's indiscretions. "We didn't know it, but she has been skipping school pretty regularly. Her school counselor called me at work one day. She called to give me the dates Pamela could make up a test in one of her classes. When I asked why Pamela needed to make up the test, the counselor told me it was because of an absence. When I told her that Pamela had not been sick in months, we both became suspicious. It turns out she had missed eleven classes over the previous six weeks. I was shocked."

Pamela grew angry when asked about her rule violations. Her anger was unbalanced, though. She was angry only because her mother was upset with her. Mrs. Penders said, "I thought she would be mad because I told the counselor we had been having similar problems with her at home. She wasn't happy about that, but the thing she honed in on was that I had no right to intervene in her school affairs. She told me that what she did at school was her business and not mine. She said that if she skipped school and her teacher didn't know about it, I was not to decide what her fate should be. Why does she think she should be immune to the rules of society?"

A spoiled teen believes that since family members make special arrangements to accommodate her whims, so should others. Not only had Pamela skipped school, she had also violated other standards of teenage behavior. These included:

- openly criticizing rules that burdened her in any way
- driving her car at whatever speed she thought was safe for her
- ignoring her friends' schedules in favor of her own
- paying others to buy beer for her even though she was a minor
- switching price tags on store items
- acting haughtily toward waiters and waitresses in restaurants
- expecting others to pay her way
- assuming she should be first in activities with her peers

Pamela was unaware of how others viewed her spoiled behavior. Behind her back her friends talked about her, using descriptive terms such as "snob," "stuck-up," "conceited," and "vain." Wearing blinders, she ignored the numerous warnings that her emotions were out of sync. Instead, she wrote off those who disagreed with her as ignorant of her special needs. She associated with other teenagers who upheld her one-sided view of life. Unfortunately, that meant joining forces with teens who had similarly skewed views of life.

Spoiled teenagers secretly harbor feelings of resentment. Outwardly they may whine, criticize, complain, or blame others. But inwardly they are disappointed with life. Hoping to find happiness in self-centeredness, the teen finds gloom instead. The teen is afraid to confront the reality that life must be shared with others. He feels it is easier to hog the spotlight than give in to the reality that we all live in a give-and-take world. Time may teach the young person that to be happy, people must live cooperatively with others. To do otherwise is a losing proposition.

Help Your Teen Take the Painful Steps toward Contentment

I hear parents say, "I know I need to teach my teenager the value of the word 'no,' but I dread the fight that will follow." Teenagers look for shortcuts that will take them right to the climax of life. A spoiled teen may accept as his motto, *I want all life has to offer, and I want it right now!* Parents know their teenager needs to live life at a more reasonable pace. Yet they would understandably love to avoid the crash that will result from putting the brakes on the teen's indulged ego.

The apostle Paul colorfully described reasons individuals should avoid a self-absorbed life. In his first letter to young Timothy, Paul details the personal qualities often found in those who are full of themselves (1 Tim. 6:3–19). Among other things they:

- know much less about life than they pretend to know
- love to fight just for the sake of fighting
- use words to stir up controversy and jealousy
- knowingly use devious tactics to get their way
- fall prey to the pitfalls of false happiness
- cause harm to themselves and others through senseless acts
- suffer one heartache after another

He cautions that those of this mind-set be taught a different set of values. Paul encourages Timothy to teach them to:

- refrain from being haughty
- abstain from a lifestyle of materialism
- be rich in service to others
- share generously what they have with others
- make a sound investment in the future by carefully living in the present

The charge Paul gave to Timothy can be duplicated for parents. Parents should hope to instill in teenagers the qualities of one who does not insist on being spoiled, but looks for ways to live cooperatively with others. That young person will find true happiness.

When Timothy read Paul's letter, he may have gulped uncomfortably when he read Paul's advice. Parents may have the same experience when told to lead spoiled teens to a more responsible view of themselves. The idea is noble, but a spoiled teen does not readily accept unsolicited counsel. He just wants to be given what he wants. "Forget the advice," he would add. Several guidelines are offered to guide the spoiled youth to a broader range of behavior:

- Go ahead and use that word you hate to utter, "no." Brace yourself for the reaction you know you will receive. By recognizing your teen's reaction as a test of your will, it will seem less offensive.
- Only offer conditions you are certain you can stick to. Avoid threats you are not likely to carry out. In fact, avoid threats as much as possible. Simply state the boundaries you are willing to stand firmly behind. Allow your teen to disagree with your guidelines. (He's going to anyway.)
- Avoid arguments with your teenager after you have drawn appropriate boundaries. Your teen knows what your opinions are, so it is not necessary to recite them. He will only use your logic and reasoning as a starting point for a verbal battle.
- Offer your teen privileges based on how responsible his behavior has been. You are not out to take away all the comforts of his life. You simply want him to put them in proper perspective.
- Keep your own lifestyle balanced. Too often parents sacrifice in order to accommodate a wanting teen. On the other hand, a spoiled teen may simply be modeling a parent who also enjoys being pampered. Live a life of moderation in which you give to others as much as you take for yourself.
- Talk openly to your teen about your desire to lead him to be more giving. Let him complain about being out of the family spotlight. Listen actively to the frustration, resentment, jealousy, or irritation he may express. Try not to give too much

unsolicited advice. Recognize that your teen will have a hard time making changes, even though they are in his best interests.

- Take the time to repair any damage that has disrupted your relationship with your teen. Spoiled teens tend to drift away from the support of those they need most—their family. Rather than wait for your teen to approach you, take the first step in rebuilding family harmony. You will be demonstrating your commitment to relationships.

◆

CHAPTER SEVENTEEN

How Am I Doing?

THE LINK BETWEEN ACHIEVEMENT AND ANGER

Think of some of your friends who have teenage children. They are men and women who have achieved varying degrees of success. Most are probably in your income bracket, some higher, others lower. Some have made significant marks in their professions while others are simply a part of the workforce. Yet all have one thing in common: Each parent is concerned about his or her relationship with a teenage child. One mother privately told me, "I wish I could succeed with my children the way I do at my job. When I'm at my office, I feel very confident in what I'm doing. When I come home, though, I'm not so sure of myself. I feel incomplete. I'm successful in one part of my life, but unsuccessful in trying to raise my two teenage children. I want to be as good at home as I am at work!"

To say that our society is driven by achievement is an understatement. Each of us is measured by our accomplishments in life. A "successful" person may have a prestigious job title, good income, country club membership, status among his peers, and a crowded calendar. We assume that this individual must also have good family relationships since so many things are going his way.

It may be true that a "successful" person may achieve success in family relationships, but one does not guarantee the other. Many parents will experience difficulties at home that run counter to their accomplishments at work. Some teens fail to meet their parents' expectations.

CASE STUDY: *Are We Having Fun?*

It was Saturday afternoon and Mr. Sanders decided to spend some time with his teenage sons, Eric and Aaron. Eric grabbed a football and tossed it to his dad as he yelled, "Hey, Dad, catch!" Caught off guard by his son's throw, Dad barely managed to duck as the ball sailed over his head. Aaron laughed and retrieved the ball.

The three horsed around a few minutes until Dad suggested, "Let's play a little game of football. I'll be the quarterback and you two guys can play against each other." Even though Eric was three years younger than his brother, the boys agreed to their dad's plan and enthusiastically began their play. Eric took the football first and tried to score against his older brother. In their small huddle Dad instructed his son, "Hike the ball and then run straight out about ten feet. Then cut sharply to your right and I'll throw you the ball."

Eric hiked the ball to his father, ran twenty feet, and cut sharply to the left. Dad threw the ball to his mixed-up teammate only to have it intercepted by Aaron who ran for a touchdown. "Hey, Dad, why didn't you stop Aaron from scoring?" called Eric.

"Because I'm not the one who messed up on the play. You turned left after twenty feet when I told you to go right after ten feet!" Dad was upset at Eric for failing to follow his instructions.

Unaware that his father was so upset, Eric kiddingly rebutted, "My fault! You were the one who threw the ball right at Aaron. How could that be my fault?"

Dad snapped, "Because you didn't do what I told you to do, that's why!" The sharpness in Dad's voice told Eric not to joke around any further.

A few minutes later Aaron became the victim of his father's pressure. As Aaron attempted to run from his younger brother, he stumbled and fell. "Oh, come on, Aaron! Can't you do better than that? You can't even run without falling down. How do you expect to win if you fall all over the place while Eric is chasing you?"

"I didn't fall on purpose, Dad," came Aaron's protest. "I just tripped. Haven't you ever tripped before?"

Teasing his son, Dad replied, "No. I learned that when you run you're supposed to put one foot in front of the other." Failing to see the humor in his father's verbal jab, Aaron dragged himself slowly back to the huddle to get instructions on the next play. "What's wrong? You can't take it when you see a little ol' boy like Eric chasing you?" Dad was hoping to push Aaron by making him mad. Instead of being motivated, however, Aaron gave less effort on the next play.

Not liking his son's sour attitude, Dad chided Aaron. "Hey, if we're going to play, let's play the right way. I didn't come out here to play with a couple of boys who pout and get mad when I tell them how they can be better. You two guys are going to have to toughen up some. You'll never get anywhere in life if you take on the kind of attitudes you guys have shown out here."

For a few minutes longer Aaron and Eric apathetically continued their play with their father. Irritated at their passive ways, Dad stopped the game and asked, "Do you two fellas want to play ball, or do you want to quit?"

"Quit," answered Eric, acting as spokesman for himself and his brother.

Shaking his head, Dad walked into the house with the football. Seeing the disgust on his face, Mrs. Sanders asked, "What happened out there? I heard you yelling at the boys."

"Nothing. That's just it. Nothing happened. I don't understand why two boys as big as those two have to act like such babies. You'd think they never learned how to follow directions or take a little constructive criticism." With a deep sigh, he added, "I don't know what it takes to teach those two to play a simple backyard game of football the right way!"

While Dad was inside complaining to his wife about his sons' poor attitudes, Eric and Aaron were holding their own conversation. "Why does Dad have to be so hard on us?" Eric asked his older brother. "You make just one mistake and he jumps on you like you're a criminal. He thinks he's doing us a favor by playing a game with us. Well, I've got something to say the next time he wants to do anything with me. I'll tell him he can play football alone."

Aaron echoed his brother's sentiment. "Yeah, he just ruined our afternoon. I don't want to go in the house now because he's probably in there telling Mom what sissies we are. He thinks he's the only one who can do anything right."

Right Expectations, Wrong Methods

Mr. Sanders's backyard encounter with his sons is typical of ways parents may attempt to push achievement on teens only to be met by teenage anger. As this father played football with Eric and Aaron, he tried to instill in them the basic qualities necessary to achieve at a higher level in life. When he fussed at Eric for running twenty feet and turning left instead of running ten feet and turning right, Mr. Sanders was attempting to teach him the value of following instructions. There's nothing wrong with that.

After Aaron stumbled and fell, allowing Eric to catch him, Dad's reprimand was meant to teach his son to avoid needless errors. Again, that message is one any youth needs to learn. The intent of Dad's words was positive, but their impact was lost somewhere along the way. Instead of teaching his sons to achieve to their maximum potential, Eric and Aaron absorbed a different set of beliefs about themselves, including:

- *I can't make the grade, so it's easier to just give in.*
- *Dad is always looking for ways he can control me. Maybe I should fight back instead of giving in to his authority.*
- *Maybe it's true that I can't do anything right. If that's the case, I'll probably keep on messing up the rest of my life.*
- *I thought I was doing pretty well. If my dad says I'm not, I must not be a good judge of my own strengths and weaknesses.*

• *I don't trust my dad when he says anything nice to me. What's his ulterior motive?*

Office Routine Fails at Home

Mr. Sanders had a responsible job as an office manager for a large company in his city. Several people worked under his direction and reported their work activities to him. He was accustomed to the trivial problems that characterize most office organizations. Whenever a problem arose, his job was to assess the situation, make a decision on how to handle it, and implement a plan of action. There were times that his coworkers disagreed with his choices, but Mr. Sanders was known as a good negotiator who did an admirable job of keeping peace among the ranks.

In a conversation with his wife, Mr. Sanders discussed his frustration with their sons' behavior. "I just don't get it. At the office when one of the owners wants a management problem solved, he comes straight to my desk to talk about it. He knows I'll get the job done because I don't put up with any of the petty behavior. I just listen to what they have to say and then I tell them what we're going to do, and it gets done.

"At home, though, a problem comes up with the boys and nothing works like it's supposed to work. I can size up the situation quickly and I usually know what the boys need to do to correct their problems. When I tell them what they need to do, though, they just argue with me. I don't like that. If they would do what I tell them to do, they'd be surprised how much easier life would be for them. I don't think I'm too tough on them. I only want what's best for them, but they don't seem to realize it."

The home requires a different formula for success than the workplace. Most occupations reward those who are competitive, even aggressive. Most employers view a quick mind that makes decisions easily as an advantage. People seem to value the ability to "get the job done" even if means stepping on a few toes. Although relationships are seen as important in the workforce, job performance takes priority over relationship development.

Many adults attempt to perform their job as parent much as they would carry out the role of a professional. As in the Sanders home, emphasis may be placed on the performance of the children, who are viewed almost as "employees." Aggressive tactics are used to push them to excel at being teenagers, however that is defined. Greater emphasis may be given to the end result of a young person's actions than to his feelings and emotions. In the same way that one worker may pull rank over another to squelch a disagreement, a parent may use power tactics to quiet a disgruntled child.

Most coworkers know the limits of their power in their job setting. Few employees will upbraid a boss since that could mean losing a job. Most workers expect that each will help the other so that goals may be reached. In the home, however, teenagers use a different standard to guide their behavior toward other family members.

Knowing that their parents will not fire them, teenagers will challenge the family power structure. Teens who feel they have a limited voice in family policies may place personal interests before family needs. Household rules will likely be ignored when the teen feels they do not meet his real needs.

Emphasize Relationships Over Rules

There is a funny irony about the relationship between family ties and teenage responsibility. The greater the emphasis on keeping rules and regulations, the more likely a teenager is to break out of the pack and define his own set of behavior standards. As families emphasize communication and togetherness, the teenager's desire to meet his parent's challenging demands grows. Even in the context of backyard play a parent can demonstrate the importance of relationships causing the teen to be drawn to the adult's leadership.

Let's recreate the backyard football scene with Mr. Sanders and his sons. In this scenario we can observe the difference that results when relationships are emphasized over achievement. As in the first case, Dad has just told Eric to hike the ball, run ten feet, and cut sharply to the right.

Counter to his father's instructions, Eric ran twenty feet and cut left. When Dad threw the ball, Aaron intercepted it and ran for a touchdown. Eric called, "Hey, Dad, why didn't you stop Aaron from scoring?"

"That Aaron is fast! I don't think I could catch him!" Trotting to Eric's side, Dad poked the young person in the ribs. "Do you think Troy Aikman's job is safe?" He ignored Eric's mistake of running the wrong pass pattern, seeing it as inconsequential.

The youth chuckled as he chided his father, "I'll say! You threw it right at Aaron."

With a broad smile on his face, Dad returned the friendly banter, "I don't think either of us has much chance of making it in the NFL." As he walked away to team up with Aaron he added, "But we'll get ol' Aaron the next time."

Moments later Aaron stumbled and fell as he was pursued by his younger brother. Dad approached the teen while he was lying on the ground. Holding out his hand, he said, "You could probably use some help getting up." As he hoisted his son to his feet he commented, "Eric's better than he used to be, isn't he?"

Not wanting to admit inferiority to his younger brother, Aaron sluffed off his father's comment. "Aw, he's just lucky I fell. He's still a kid."

When play continued, Dad commented to his sons, "We may not be the world's greatest athletes, but there's one thing we can say about the Sanders boys—we sure do know how to have fun!" Both teens acknowledged their dad's comment. The three continued their play until Dad quit in exhaustion a half hour later.

In this illustration, Eric and Aaron's emotional state was different than in the first scenario. Their dad did not leave them to wallow in anger. The boys' need for affirmation had been met by a father who realized the importance of healthy family relationships. In this case, Mr. Sanders had not abandoned his belief that his sons needed to achieve their potential. The emphasis he gave to the boys' emotional well-being *increased* the likelihood that they would push themselves to be all they were capable of being. Consider what Eric and Aaron might have assumed about themselves following this positive exchange with their dad:

- *I may not be perfect, but that's no reason to keep from playing the game.*
- *Dad knows what it's like to be like me. That quality in him makes me want to cooperate when he has to show his authority.*
- *Dad doesn't place too much emphasis on what I do wrong. That encourages me to keep trying to improve.*
- *It's not what I achieve that makes me a good person. My ability to relate to others makes me feel good about myself.*
- *I can trust my dad when he says nice things to me. His only motive is to show me that he loves me.*

Even though Eric and Aaron's performance while they played football with their dad was not emphasized, the conclusions they were able to draw about themselves increased the possibility that they would become the achievers their parents wanted them to be. Mr. Sanders shifted gears from a no-nonsense office manager to the role of a father who met the demands of family life.

In the workforce, achievement is often related to the adult's ability to tackle problems successfully. In family life, parents foster a young person's achievement when they focus on the young person's ability to grow into all he is capable of being. Family interaction that tolerates mistakes, compliments effort, and emhasizes the worth of each member encourages a teen to reach his potential.

CHAPTER EIGHTEEN

◆

Watch, Learn, Act

SIMMERING ANGER MAY EMERGE IN ADOLESCENCE

A proud father told a group of friends a cute story illustrating how his five-year-old daughter loved to imitate her mother. "Last Saturday Marie made a cake to take to a dinner party later that evening. Heather was playing in the kitchen while Marie was busy measuring all the ingredients, mixing them up, pouring the batter into the cake pan, and so on. She didn't know that Heather was watching her so closely.

"The next morning Heather got up earlier than the rest of us and made her way to the kitchen to bake a cake of her own. I happened to hear her just in time to prevent a disaster. When I went into the kitchen I found Heather sitting on the floor pouring her 'cake batter' into a bowl. She had already turned the oven up as high as it would go and was going to bake the batter she had whipped up. You'll never guess the ingredients in this cake. She had mixed together laundry detergent, sugar, salt, barbeque sauce, and chocolate chips. Don't ask me what kind of cake she was making. Maybe she thought her mother's cake tasted like it must have had those things in it.

"I caught her just before she put the bowl full of that awful mess into the oven. She cried and couldn't understand why I wouldn't let her finish baking her cake. She said that since we didn't have any cake left from the day before, she wanted to make one for our Sunday dessert."

This amusing story illustrates how children imitate their parents' actions. In recent years, the parent's influence as a role model for

175

children has attracted the attention of psychologists. The consensus of opinion is that while children have their own personality style, parents have a strong influence in the way that inborn personality is expressed.

We parents are often unaware of how we show our children unbalanced behaviors and emotions. A wife chided her husband for his use of surly language in the presence of their children. This proud man retorted, "I don't see why you're so concerned about me having a bad influence on the kids. I've never once heard them use rough language. They know when I'm mad. They know that I'm just spouting off when I talk like that. That doesn't mean they're going to act just like I do when they get mad. They'll find their own way to show their anger."

It is true that children do not immediately imitate all of their parents' behaviors. In fact, many children purposely decide *not* to act like their parents. Nonetheless, the teenager sometimes shows how much he has learned through imitation.

Teenagers Recall Imitated Behaviors Years Later

Children are constantly in a state of learning, whether we recognize it or not. They absorb subtle lessons about how we adults handle our emotions. Often it is not until adolescence that young people show what they have learned from their parents about emotional control.

CASE STUDY: *Following in Daddy's Footsteps*

Beth described herself as an abused child. "As far back as I can remember, I was abused, especially by my father. If I did something that was just the least bit wrong, I got whipped. Daddy said he was trying to teach me right from wrong. He can say what he wants to about what he did to me. I say it was abuse."

"But when you were a child, you never stood up to your dad. I suppose you weren't in a position to defend yourself."

"What *could* I have done? My daddy was a lot bigger than I was. I couldn't do anything but take it. Sometimes I would get mad and yell at him, but that just made things worse. I remember my mother telling me that God would punish daddy some day for the way he treated me. She tried to talk to him, but he wouldn't listen to anybody, not even Mother. I used to wish God would hurry up and punish Daddy so he would start acting nicer to me."

"I'll bet you've given up hope that change will happen."

"I gave up a long time ago. My mother says I'm starting to act just like my father, but there's no way I'll ever be like he is. I don't hit people who don't deserve it and then call it discipline."

"You must do something that reminds your mother of your father."

"She says I'm becoming mean-spirited. That's the word she uses to describe me now. I'm not mean-spirited. I'm just tired of taking all this stuff off of people and not giving any in return. I'm just defending myself."

"It must be working for you."

"Well, my daddy doesn't spank me anymore. He doesn't yell as long as he used to yell. He knows that if he pushes me too far, he's going to lose his daughter. I'm gone if he goes back to his old ways— and he knows it!"

Beth's last comment hinted at how she had learned from her father to use her anger. She was imitating his negative behaviors more than she cared to admit. Teenagers have a tendency to rationalize their own anger more than that of others. Let's look at the learning process that eventually lead Beth to act like her father.

- As a young child Beth watched as her father overpowered the family physically and emotionally.
- Beth noted that her father's angry explosions resulted in the control of the family. She did not like the way he captured power, but felt helpless to counteract his behavior.

177

- Beth's mother tried to punish Beth's father by verbally chastising him. She hoped Beth would learn that her father's impulsive anger was inappropriate. She assumed the child would see the error of her father's explosions.
- To her mother's dismay, Beth showed the effects of her earlier abusive experiences by displaying the same calloused and forceful anger her father had shown years earlier.

Beth's mother had assumed that since the child did not show the same impulsive anger as her father when she was young, she never would. In reality, Beth simply waited until adolescence to demonstrate what she learned years earlier. As you can imagine, Mother was distraught that the lessons she had taught Beth about anger control had apparently gone unheeded. She did not understand why Beth's anger did not surge until adolescence.

At one point Beth's mother commented, "I thought I had succeeded in teaching Beth to control her anger. When she was young I tried to teach her that just because her father acted the way he did, she had no reason to imitate him. If I had known she had been feeling this angry all these years, maybe I could have done something about it. I don't understand why she waited until she was fifteen to show her anger. I feel that it's almost too late now to help her."

Teens Show What They Have Learned

There are numerous reasons teenagers might delay the expression of feelings that have simmered for years. Many teens wait until they are older to show their feelings because they could not put words to their feelings earlier. Or, the teen's peer group may encourage him to assert himself more forcefully.

One overlooked factor explains why teenage anger is sometimes more potent than pre-adolescent or childhood anger: *It is not until adolescence that many teenagers learn that their anger can be rewarded.* Here's how Beth expressed it:

"I got to thinking one day that my dad has been controlling this family for years just because nobody will stand up to him. Everyone was scared of him because he would make awful threats when we tried to put him down. Sometimes he backed up his threats with a good beating. I figured that if my dad could threaten me, I could threaten him, too. So I did."

"You mean, you wanted to have something to show for your anger just like your dad had something to show for his."

"Right. Here he had all this power over the family and I had none. At least I thought I had none. That's because I wasn't fighting back."

"So you fought back in order to get a reward." Beth nodded her head. "What were those rewards?" Beth named several. They included:

- *If I feel frustrated, it feels good to take someone down with me. That way I feel that we're even.*
- *Even though it sounds mean to say it, I like it when my dad doesn't know what to do with me. That means he's not running my life.*
- *I've learned that when you back people down, they're more likely to give in. I get to do more things now because my parents don't want to fight with me.*
- *My friends tell me they wish they had the nerve to stand up for themselves the way I do. My best friend tells me all the time that she's proud of me.*
- *You may not believe it, but I actually feel better about myself than I used to. I don't sit around and feel sorry for myself like I did when I was younger.*

Beth's anger demonstrated that she had, indeed, learned from her childhood experiences at the hands of an angry parent. It was

179

not until the circumstances were right, though, that she displayed an imitation of her father's angry pose.

There are two phases of imitated learning. The first phase is when the child observes others' behavior, learning how different acts are rewarded or punished. In the second phase the young person acts out what he has observed. It may be years, as in Beth's case, before the child feels that the circumstances are ripe to display his learning. The young person may also wait until she sees enough rewards awaiting her to make it worthwhile to angrily blast others. But, we should make no mistake that children are constantly learning as they observe our adult behavior.

Adults and Teens Can Learn Together

A teenager like Beth obviously needed to learn to manage manipulative anger. Her rationalization that she was only responding to her father as he treated her was a weak excuse for her misguided behavior. We all know the old saying that "two wrongs don't make a right." Beth knew it, too, but she found it easy to ignore that simple guideline.

During a joint meeting with Beth and her parents, the teenager unloaded on her parents. "Neither one of you cares one bit about me! If you did, you would treat me better. Daddy, you're always saying you treat me hard to discipline me, but all you're really doing is driving me away from you. You're so hard on me that I refuse to even listen to what you're trying to tell me! And Mother, you try to tell me not to be so upset—just ignore the things that go on at home. Well, that might work for you, but it doesn't work for me! I can't ignore it when I get beat down all the time. I'm going to keep standing up for myself because if I don't, I'll end up being a nobody. And I can't stand that thought!"

For a brief moment the family sat quietly, each one staring at the floor. That awkward moment seemed to last an eternity. The room was full of tension, but the parents' silence gave Beth hope that her message had been heard. To her shock and delight, Beth's dad broke the silence with a simple, but conciliatory, statement. "I never really took time to look at what your mother and I have done to you." That was all the man could say, but the very fact that he did not retaliate against his daughter's anger spoke volumes to the girl.

After another pause, I commented, "This family knows that anger has strangled family relationships for years."

Dad spoke up again. "There's a part of me that wants to blast a teenage girl who would talk to me and her mother like Beth just did. But there's another part of me that's just plain tired of trying to force my daughter to act the right way. If my way of disciplining the kids is wrong, I want to know what I should do that's better."

I responded, "We can look to Beth for some thoughts on that question. She has a lot of ideas about what the family can do to get along better."

The girl who was so bold moments earlier suddenly became meek. She was not prepared to suggest how the family could improve relations. She had come to the meeting with the intention of blowing her parents through the wall with her anger. She stammered as she searched for the right words to say. "I don't know. I guess for a start we could spend more time talking with each other instead of shouting. I don't like it when we argue all the time. I'd like that to stop."

The girl who'd sat on the edge of her seat screaming just minutes earlier was now a picture of politeness. Underneath her anger was a desire to communicate more openly with her parents. The irony of her sentiment was that her father and mother had the same wish. "That would be nice," whispered her mother. Dad nodded his agreement.

Though wanting to believe her parents were sincere, Beth still had doubts about their willingness to change, especially her overpowering father. With a question mark in her eyes, Beth commented to her father, "But why did you treat me so hard for so long? Did you really think it would make me want to obey you?"

Dad shrugged his shoulders. "You didn't get it any worse than I did when I was a kid. I hoped you would understand what I was trying to teach you. I guess I taught you the wrong thing. Your mother tells me the same thing she tells you. You're getting to be just like me." Dad smiled as Beth rolled her eyes.

For the remainder of that hour, the family members talked about some of their mutual frustrations and hurts in a way they had not talked in years. Both teenager and adults knew they were being heard. Being understood felt good to everyone.

The news that teens imitate their parents' emotions does not have to be bad news. During the span of one quick hour, Beth followed her parents' willingness to rethink their communication with her. She readily imitated their stance of emotional moderation and generated workable solutions to family problems.

In the same way children model the angry expressions of adults, they can also imitate adult growth. In fact, young people model positive adult behavior more quickly than they model negative behavior. Remember, children and teenagers constantly watch adults for cues on how to respond to the inescapable stresses of life.

A senior adult friend of mine, who was short on formal education but long on wisdom, talked about his role in influencing young people: "I figured out a long time ago that whether I like it or not, I'm going to make a mark on kids. I also figured that I'm never the same one day as I was the day before. I keep changing just like everybody else. It makes sense that when we walk down life's road, we take someone along with us to make the journey pleasant. I try not to judge kids, or analyze them, or tell them they can't be who they really are. That way they're more likely to do what I do, listen to what I say, and act the way I think they should act. And the good part is that I always have a companion to go with me through life!"

At times the best response to simple wisdom is to utter "Amen" and say no more.

◆

CHAPTER NINETEEN

The Peer Group Takes Aim

PEER PRESSURE TAKES ITS TOLL ON TEENS

It is ironic how the thoughts of teenagers and their parents are often parallel. When asked to name the greatest problem facing teenagers today, most parents will place peer pressure at the top of the list. They will say that peer pressure is a primary cause of drug use, sexual promiscuity, crime, rebellion, and a host of other problems. These parents are right, for peer pressure *is* a root cause for many of these problems.

Even though we often think of parents and teenagers as being on different wavelengths, teens usually agree with parents on this issue. When adolescents are asked to name the greatest problem they face today, most will identify peer pressure as a major concern. They agree with their parents that drug use, sexual promiscuity, crime, and teen defiance is fueled by peer pressure.

With parents and teens in agreement that something should be done to reduce negative peer pressure, it seems that this problem should be solved in short order. Unfortunately, the issue of teen peer pressure does not have a simple solution. Parents and teens see this problem in a different light.

During a parenting conference, I invited several teenagers to join the group in a discussion of family problems. The subject of peer pressure came up. Disagreements between the two groups were evident, though, when parents were asked to assess how strongly their own teenagers were affected by this pressure. The parents believed their children's behavior was strongly influenced by their

185

peers. The teens, while acknowledging the damage done by peer pressure, said that *other* teenagers, not themselves, were affected by this problem. Most teens see themselves as relatively immune to the pressures the peer group places on them. Some statements commonly made by young people include:

- *I didn't do it because everybody else was doing it. I did it because I wanted to.*
- *I know what my limits are. I can say no anytime I want.*
- *Believe me when I say I've thought through my decision. I know what I'm getting into.*
- *My friends wouldn't talk me into doing something they know is not good for me. We're not getting into something that's over our head.*
- *I know the difference between right and wrong. I know what I believe in.*

Peer Pressure Is Fueled by Dependency

Teenagers want very badly to be seen as independent. The next time you are in public, look for families with teenagers. (That may be a tough task since most teenagers prefer to be somewhere besides out with their family.) Notice how the teen often sets himself apart from his parents. A teenager may dress differently from the other family members. She may keep a distance between herself and the family. He may not engage in ready conversation with the family. His eyes may roll when his parents act so, so—adult-like! All these behaviors make the statement, *I want to be independent.*

Or do they? Teenagers are far more dependent than they admit. We have discussed how teens depend on their parents. Similarly, the young person is dependent on the peer group. Generally, this dependence is by choice, but the teen is still dependent—despite assertions of independence! When the teen dresses differently, distances himself, withholds conversation, or experiences embarrassment over adults, he is not stating a desire to be completely independent. He is simply saying, *I want to be independent of my family, but I still need a group I can cling to.*

One way teenagers satisfy their need for independence is through an *overidentification* with their peers. They may refer to themselves as emotionally independent because they are no longer as attached to their family as they once were. A quick inspection of their relationships with other teens reveals just how dependent they are, though. In the parenting seminar mentioned earlier, one teenager looked to the teen on her right before answering the question, "Are *you* strongly influenced by peer pressure?" After seeing the youth next to her shake her head no, she also responded negatively.

Peer pressure is not bad. One reason teenagers fail to recognize their dependence on their peer group is that peer pressure gets a great deal of bad publicity. But it is a fact of life that peer pressure begins to affect each of us during early childhood and continues into adult life. It simply reaches a climax during adolescence.

The Peer Group Answers Teens' Questions

Teenagers are full of questions. Adolescence marks a time when teens are capable of asking questions for the first time. Questions such as:

- *Who am I, anyway? What kind of person will I be?*
- *Who is God? Do I have a relationship with Him? How can I make sense of the spiritual world?*
- *What makes me feel the way I do physically? What's happening to my body? What do I do with my physical impulses?*
- *What am I good at? Is it true what others say about me? What's my opinion of myself?*
- *What stance will I take on social issues? Political matters? Why do people believe the way they do?*

• *Do I have any real power in this world? What difference can one person make?*

These questions can be overpowering to the teenager. Teens tend to look to other teens for answers. Too often we adults try to impose our own answers on teens' difficult questions. Or, we may ignore the teenager's struggle with life since we do not share his intense concerns. Hoping to find understanding from someone, teenagers look to their peers for both affirmation and answers. It is as if one teen says to another, *I've got a lot of questions about life that I don't understand. Do you feel the same way I feel? What do you think about all these things? Let's search together.*

Teenagers find security in knowing they are not alone as they struggle to find their niche in the world. It is, then, natural that they would look for solutions to their questions from those who share their plight. As youth attempt to make sense of themselves, they build alliances with one another. They may isolate themselves from adults who can offer guidance through certain hard times. They may become aggressive as they try to force answers on life. They may allow themselves to be dominated by the prevailing winds of their social world.

In this search for personal understanding the teenager may insist that he is acting independently, free from peer pressure, even though he is not. The young person is hard to understand. Parents often complain that they do not know their own child anymore. This is the misunderstanding that drives wedges between parents and teenagers.

Teens Still Need to Be Bonded to Their Parents

Many parents have difficulty understanding a teenager who thinks so differently than they do. One parent expressed what so many others feel when she said, "I think I understand why my daughter does what she does. I'm afraid, though, that if I *tell* her I understand she'll think I agree with her and nothing could be further from the truth." This fear that we will push our teenagers to self-destruction if we show understanding often keeps us from helpful communication.

Instead of taking the risk of encouraging teenage mistakes, we often take what appears to be the safe road of pointing out to the teenager how he *should* think and feel. By offering him the advantage of their experience in life, parents hope to prevent teen mistakes. Yet, teenagers need the assurance that their parents understand the depth of those yet-unanswered questions about life. Teenagers tend to reject parental guidance that is not preceded by understanding.

CASE STUDY: *Josh's Rumpled Shirt*

Josh was in his bedroom getting ready to go out for the evening. He had plans to take his girlfriend, Peggy, to a movie. Afterward, he and Peggy would meet at one of their friend's house for snacks and games. As he combed his hair, his dad looked in the doorway. "What time are you supposed to pick Peggy up, Josh?"

"Seven o'clock."

"It's almost seven now. Don't you think you need to get moving?" As Dad spoke, he noticed a puzzled look on his son's face. "What's wrong? You look like you're thinking about something."

Josh sighed as he asked his dad, "Do you think this shirt looks alright? I can't decide if it goes with these pants."

Dad laughed lightly at Josh's question. The shirt Josh was wearing was wrinkled, looking as if it had been crumpled in the back of a drawer. In his mind the question should not have been whether the shirt and pants matched. Dad wondered why Josh would want to wear that shirt at all. "If you want my opinion, Josh, I'd get rid of that shirt. It doesn't look good with any pants."

Josh pretended not to hear his father as he looked at himself in the mirror. Satisfied with what he saw, he replied, "No. It looks fine. This shirt is supposed to look like this. That's the way it was designed. I guess it goes with these pants. Anyway, Peggy gave it to me. She'd like it if I wore it tonight."

Dad had a hard time keeping his feelings to himself. "You've got to be kidding. Peggy thinks that shirt looks good? I thought she had pretty good taste. Maybe she's not the sensible girl I thought she was. If you ask me, I think it needs to be ironed. I know I wouldn't be caught wearing a shirt that looked like that."

Josh kept his thoughts private, but inwardly mused, *I didn't ask you what you thought. I don't care what your opinion is. What's more, Peggy is a sensible girl. She's got a lot more sense than you have.* Josh hurriedly put on his shoes and said nothing as his dad watched. Rushing through the doorway, Josh curtly bade his dad good-bye. "I'll see you later, Dad. I gotta run. I'll be home later."

As Josh hurried through the house, he passed his mother in the hallway. Noticing his crumpled shirt, she unknowingly added fuel to Josh's internal fire. "Josh, don't you need to iron that shirt before you rush out of here?"

The teen failed to look back as he mumbled to himself, "What's the big deal with this shirt? Doesn't anybody around here know what's in style these days? I should have never asked Dad to help me decide what to wear. What does he know? And why does Mom always have to butt in and repeat what Dad has just said?" Not wanting to ignore his mother completely, he called out as he walked out the door, "I look fine, Mom. Don't worry about me. I can take care of myself."

After Josh picked up Peggy at her house, she complimented his choice of clothes. "I like that shirt, Josh. It looks good on you."

"I wish you'd tell my parents that. No, on second thought, you'd better not. They both said that this shirt looks bad. When I told them you liked it, they put you in the same category as me. They think both of us lack taste and intelligence."

Peggy reacted, "Oh, don't worry about what they say. Parents are like that. They have no idea what it's like to be a teenager. Just do what I do and ignore what your parents say and you'll be alright." Josh and Peggy laughed at his parents' ignorance about style.

Later that evening Josh and Peggy were at their friend Tom's house. A group of about ten teenagers was listening to a stereo while they played a game. To say they were making a lot of noise was an understatement. To Tom's dismay, his father walked into the room, turned down the stereo, turned around, and walked out of the room. As he left, he stated, "Tom, you all need to tone it down."

Feeling embarrassed, Tom apologized to his friends after his father left the room. "Sorry. My dad's just like that. He doesn't know what it's like to have fun. He thinks that you can only have fun if everything's real quiet. He tells me to pipe down all the time."

Hoping to console Tom, Peggy spoke up. "Hey, don't worry about it, Tom. Your dad's no different from the rest of the adults." Everyone shook their heads as Peggy continued. "Josh's parents are the same way. They think his shirt looks bad, and they think I'm a bimbo because I happen to like it. My parents are the same, too. My mom tells me all the time what she thinks is good for me, even though she doesn't have a clue about what I need."

Each youth agreed with Peggy's sentiments. They either nodded their head, added a cutting statement about adults, or poked fun at the backward way most parents think. Buoyed that they had successfully repelled the negative impact of adult thinking, the teens continued in their fun.

This kind of encounter encourages teenagers to turn from their parents to their peer group for guidance through life. Though it seems that this group of teenagers was only minimally damaged by their encounters with adults, repeated empty conversations between teenagers and their parents push the parent from a position of influence in the teen's life. As teenagers discuss their mutual feelings of misunderstanding by their parents, they become increasingly dependent on one another. Not only do teens seek affirmation from their peer group about minor matters such as personal dress or social manners, they look to one another for direction on matters with more serious implications.

Parents would do well to recognize that teen reliance on the peer group moves him closer to responsible adult living. Rather than block the teen's effort to shed his dependence on the family, parents are in a position to help the growing, but still immature, young person. Parents can stay connected with their teenager. Teens need not drift too far from the wisdom of adults to a negative peer group. Some guidelines are as follows:

- Recognize that a teenager needs a separate identity from his parents as he becomes his own person. Overreacting to the teen's need to try different roles only pushes him to continue to be different, if for no other reason than to make a stronger statement of independence.
- Continue to be a part of your teenager's support system. Even though the opinion of other teenagers is ultimately important, your opinion will continue to count if you show an awareness of your teen's positive qualities. Make a point of frequently complimenting your teen.
- Refrain from giving your opinion on relatively unimportant matters until your teenager asks for your views or is obviously open to your comments. Focus on showing your teenager you understand him. He will not mistake your understanding for agreement. Teens know their parents well enough to know their opinion on virtually any topic. As you demonstrate a willingness to listen to your teen, he will ask for your advice more frequently.
- Gradually ease parental controls. When parents refuse to give control to teenagers, rebellion is increasingly likely. Rebellious teens do not trust adults and feel they have no one to turn to for direction but their peer group. Conversely, when parents give up control too quickly, teens tend to weave through adoles-

cence like a runaway train. The teen may say he's having fun in life, but his lifestyle of reckless abandon will come to a screeching halt some day.

- Recognize that healthy communication is your best tool in building a powerful relationship with your teenager. As you talk with your teen about things of interest to him, the conversation will often drift to topics that have eternal significance. Well-timed comments, spoken with tact and understanding, leave a lasting impression on the teenager. Teens are quick to accept the views of a parent who communicates with acceptance and understanding.
- Live a lifestyle that shows your teen what it means to be personally, socially, and spiritually fulfilled. Teenagers notice authentic traits of happiness in adults. They will want to know how to find that contentment. Young people who come from families that are well-rooted are less likely to try to look for shortcuts to happiness.

THE PARENT RESPONDS TO THE ANGRY TEEN

CHAPTER TWENTY

◆

What Am I Supposed to Say?

OPEN COMMUNICATION CAN DIFFUSE TEEN ANGER

S o what am I supposed to say to my son when he's as angry as a wet hen? Am I supposed to just pretend it isn't there? And what about my own anger? I can't just keep it bottled up inside all the time. What do I do with *my* feelings? Is it a sin to be angry at my kids when they've done something wrong?"

A mother spoke these words to a friend as she struggled to understand her two children. She was perplexed. She only wanted her children to control their angry emotions, a simple desire. She knew she was the single most influential role model in their lives. Still she could not find the best way to teach her teenage children how to handle anger.

We have learned that anger takes many shapes and forms. Angry feelings can range from simple emotional discomfort to blind rage. Anger can create tremendous tension in a young person, even to the point of physical illness. Anger can destroy relationships. Anger can turn on the teen and create almost unbearable loneliness and depression. It is little wonder, then, that this mother felt so confused about her role as teacher and counselor to her children. All parents want to do their part to make sure this potentially deadly emotion is kept in its proper place in the teenager's emotional arsenal.

Why Do We Say What We Say?

Despite a parent's best intention to control family anger, sometimes anger wins the battle. I have yet to meet a parent who has not experienced the frustration of giving in to anger's destructive urge. At times we can only shake our heads in frustration and admit that we do not know what to say to an angry teenager.

There is a reason for everything we say and do. As we examine ourselves honestly, we often find that our response to anger reflects how we learned to handle this emotion. Remember, most people consider anger to be a "negative" emotion, one that has no place in a healthy family. Looking back on our own histories as children and teenagers, the majority of us can remember hearing some of the following messages from our parents:

- from an overpowering father: *You've got no right to talk that way to me! Just what makes you think you can get away with that kind of disrespect?*
- from a worrisome mother: *Just try to keep your feelings to yourself. If you keep letting everybody know how upset you are, you'll lose all your friends.*
- from a passive-aggressive parent: *(glaring) Go to your room. We don't talk like that around here. (Refuses to talk to child the remainder of the evening.)*
- from an overly sensitive mother: *You don't really mean that, do you? Just give your brother a hug and let him know you love him. That will get rid of your angry feelings.*
- from an apathetic father: *Oh, let them fight it out. One of these days they'll learn that it doesn't do any good to argue the way they do.*
- from a denying parent: *You say you're mad, but don't you really think you're just trying to get some attention? Nobody could be as upset as you are over such an insignificant thing.*

One task of adulthood is to examine our pasts to understand why we act and feel the way we do. As we review messages we received about anger, there is little wonder we grope for the right response to our children's anger. Most adults were given a single childhood message about this emotion: *Anger is wrong!* Having been taught to feel guilty, resentful, embarrassed, or even sinful because of our angry feelings, we send the same message to our own children. As adults we may have heard that anger is not a bad emotion, but echoes from the past bid us to deny the reality that it is.

CASE STUDY: *Trey's "Bad Attitude"*

Trey sat quietly in my office as his parents talked about their typical response to his mistakes. "Well," began his mother, "whenever Trey makes a mistake, I try to correct him. I want to teach him the difference between right and wrong." His father added, "We feel that it's our job to teach him to use his feelings in the right way."

"That makes sense," I said. "Of course parents should help a teenager make sense of his emotions. But somehow, it seems that Trey isn't learning all the things you want him to learn." I looked directly at Trey. He was dressed in dirty clothes, his hair uncombed. He was the exact opposite of his well-groomed, mannerly parents. "Trey, what are you learning from your parents?"

Trey grunted. "I don't know." After a pause he added, "I stay mad at them a lot of the time." Trey looked only at me and not at his mother or father.

"How's that?"

Giving an example, Trey related, "The other day I was just sitting in my room and my mom comes in and says something to me. I couldn't hear her because I had a headset on. She thought I was ignoring her because what she had said was for me to take out the trash. The next thing I know, I'm getting this lecture on how I need to be more responsible. Then I did ignore her because I didn't think I deserved a lecture just because I couldn't hear what she had said. When my dad got home, Mom told him that I had a bad attitude, so I heard it from him, too. That's why I stay mad so much of the time. No one ever really knows what's going on inside me, even though they think they do."

"You mean, they were talking to you about controlling your bad attitude, but you didn't really have a bad attitude . . ."

Trey finished the sentence, ". . . not until I was accused of having one! I'll admit I had a bad attitude after that."

Trey's mother added, "I just know that when I was a teenager and my mother told me to do something, I didn't question her or talk back to her. I knew I had better keep my feelings to myself."

Trying to determine how her childhood experiences influenced her communication with Trey, I asked, "You mean Trey should keep his feelings to himself in the same way you did?"

"I'd like him to. That would certainly save us a lot of arguments."

Trey disagreed with his mother's rationale. "I don't think so. If I kept my feelings to myself, I'd hate to think of what would happen once they did come out." Trey's comment showed he had discovered a truth about human emotions. He had learned that ignoring feelings cannot cause them to disappear.

"In other words, Trey, you need to express yourself whenever you feel frustration, irritation, rage, or any other feeling."

"Yeah. You can bet that I'm going to express myself. I don't care how I feel. I just want to be understood."

The parents' intentions were reasonable. They wanted Trey to be considerate of them and to fulfill the simple responsibilities required of any teenage son. He, in turn, wanted to be understood and treated with dignity and respect. In Trey's example of the typical problems in his home, neither parent nor teen was satisfied.

Anger stood squarely in the way of this family's satisfaction. Trey became angry because his mother mistakenly thought he had a bad attitude. Seeing that he was angry, Mother and Father took turns trying to talk him out of his feelings. Their reaction was born, in part, out of their own childhood experiences that sent the message, *Do whatever you have to do to get rid of your anger.*

Openly Recognize Anger's Presence

I continued to focus on Trey. "Trey, let's stick with the example you gave of how you can get angry at your parents. When your mother came to your room to ask you to take out the trash and wound up arguing with you over a bad attitude, what would have been a more helpful response to you?"

Trey's quick answer suggested he had already thought of that question. "It would be nice if my mother had said she was sorry for accusing me of something that wasn't true."

I clarified what he said. "You mean you got mad and stayed mad because you felt misunderstood?"

"Yes, sir."

"So you showed it by pouting and showing your mom that you were capable of having the very attitude she accused you of having."

Trey almost smiled at the irony of what I had said. "I suppose so."

"And then when your dad came home and learned how you had been rude to your mom, he became mad and fussed at you, too." Trey nodded his head.

Trey's father spoke up, "I have to admit that I have a hard time holding my anger. When I came home and Gina told me how Trey had ignored her when she tried to talk with him, that did something to me. I can't stand it when a child is impolite to his parents. I try not to say anything, but the more I try to keep it to myself, the worse the explosion is going to be when it happens."

"And that's just part of our problem here," I replied. "You *don't* have to keep your feelings to yourself. When anyone in this family feels angry about anything—because of being misunderstood, or insulted, or treated rudely—it's alright to talk about it. It's important, though, to express these feelings the right way."

Each family member changed facial expressions. Trey had assumed that yet another adult would tell him that he was wrong to become angry over a seemingly insignificant matter. The teen had hoped I would tell his parents to "lay off" of him. His parents had assumed I would counsel them not to feel angry at their son. None expected to be told to continue in their anger. That thought ran against the grain of all they had been taught in the past.

When trying to decide what to say in the face of anger, our first task is to openly recognize that it exists! Anger has a purpose. Trey's anger indicated his need to be more fully understood. His parents' anger signalled a desire for respect. By showing his irritation through a bad attitude, Trey was ensuring that the barrier between himself and his parents stood tall. His parents' anger suggested they were not indifferent to their son. They merely wanted him to learn to handle relationships effectively. But by pronouncing him guilty of an attitude he felt forced to assume, they missed his need for understanding.

By encouraging family members to openly voice their anger, I am not suggesting that teenagers and their parents take turns blasting one another with unbridled emotions. I *am* suggesting that teens be allowed to say, "This is the way I feel at this moment" and that parents be allowed to state, "These are the boundaries within which we expect you to act." The point is that anger be directly confronted in family life.

How to Talk about Angry Feelings

When families learn to talk openly about their anger, several simple rules apply:

1. Each family member must accept anger as a natural part of family communication.
2. Angry statements should stick to the problem and stay clear of character assassination.
3. The parent leads the family, thus the parent must set the boundaries for healthy communication.

4. Time should be allowed for angry feelings to pass. To demand that they go away quickly denies a person's right to feel angry.

Let's take several scenarios and offer potentially ineffective and effective parent responses:

SITUATION: Rachael's parents are going away for a couple of hours. They ask her to water the outdoor plants while they are gone. When Mom and Dad return, Rachael is asleep in front of the TV. The outdoor plants are dry, evidence that the teen failed to perform her simple job.

INEFFECTIVE REACTION: Shaking Rachael from her slumber, Dad gripes, "What have you been doing while we've been gone? Is sleeping all you ever do? Why couldn't you get off that couch for just a few minutes and water the plants like your mother asked you?" After hearing a puny excuse from Rachael, Mother adds, "That's not a good enough explanation. Now get out there and water those plants like I told you two hours ago—and you can forget about watching TV tonight!"

EFFECTIVE REACTION: Shaking Rachael from her slumber, Dad comments to Rachael, "Looks like you've been asleep for awhile. You didn't get around to watering the plants like Mom asked you to do." Rachael offers a weak excuse for her neglect, to which neither parent offers a comment. They realize that their job is to see to it that Rachael follows through with her duty. They prefer not to quibble over why it had not been done. Once she completes her task, Mom commented, "Thanks, Rachael. I appreciate your watering the plants for me." Smiling, she adds, "I'd appreciate it even more if you would do things when you were asked instead of having to be reminded."

SITUATION: Because he had repeatedly violated his mother's rule about using the telephone late at night, Eddie's mother removed his phone from his room and told him he could have it back in two weeks. Unwilling to endure two weeks without a phone, Eddie discovered where it had been hidden. He sneaked it into his room one night after his mother had gone to bed. Hearing Eddie laughing at midnight, Mom entered his room to find him talking beneath the sheets on the forbidden phone.

INEFFECTIVE REACTION: Shouting loud enough to wake up the household, Mom demands, "Give me that phone! I've told you it is off limits for two weeks and here you are talking on it after two days. Where did you get that thing anyway? Have you been rummaging through my closet? Well, you can forget about talking on the phone anytime soon. I'm keeping it for four weeks now!"

Not wanting his friend to hear his mother's tantrum, Eddie covers the mouthpiece and says, "Mom, stop yelling. You're embarrassing me!"

Mom replies, "Embarrassing you! You *should* be embarrassed. You can't even follow a simple rule!"

EFFECTIVE RESPONSE: Upon hearing Eddie laughing on the phone, Mom enters his room, catching him red-handed as he violates their agreement. Walking to the side of the bed, Mom holds out her hand and silently signals for the phone. Seeing that he has been caught, Eddie hands over the contraband and rolls over so his mom cannot look into his eyes. "We'll talk about this later," Mom says as she takes the phone and goes back to bed.

The next day Mom brings up the dreaded subject. "It's hard for you to stay away from the phone late at night, isn't it?" Getting no response from Eddie, Mom adds, "I'm disappointed that you risked getting caught just to do what you wanted to do."

Wanting to know just how much his mistake would cost him, Eddie asks, "Does this mean I don't get my phone back in two weeks?"

Mom answers, "Mistakes like that don't help your cause. I'll

wait to see how you act over the next two weeks before I decide."
Mother's intent was to keep the focus on Eddie's need to act
responsibly. She wanted to avoid encouraging further deceit or
power struggles by being too condemning or by negotiating her
position with him.

SITUATION: Thirteen-year-old Jamie went, with permission from
her parents, to a movie with a girlfriend. While the girls were at
the theater, the friend's mother called Jamie's mother and asked,
"Did you know that Missy and Jamie were meeting two boys at
the theater?" Jamie's mother said she did not. Jamie had "conve-
niently" forgotten to mention that detail. Both moms agreed that
the whole arrangement was too much like a date and felt that
their girls were too young for this kind of activity.

INEFFECTIVE REACTION: Jamie's mom arrived at the theater early
to pick up Jamie and her girlfriend. Getting out of the car, Mom
waited for the two girls to come out with their boyfriends. A
startled Jamie was confronted by her upset mother who told her,
"Tell your friends good-bye. I'm taking you two girls home."

Once they were home, Mom told her humiliated daughter
that she was too young to be going on unescorted outings with
boys. Only concerned about defending herself, Jamie listened
little and argued a lot.

EFFECTIVE RESPONSE: Jamie's mom waited in the parking lot of
the theater to pick up Jamie and her friend, just as she had said
she would. Of course, by the time they were in her mother's
sight, they had parted ways with their boyfriends. Once home,
Mom calmly explained that she and Missy's mother had talked
on the phone. Knowing that Jamie would be defensive just after
being caught in a lie, the mother said they would talk about the
situation in more detail later. The next day, when Jamie was not
as upset, Mom explained her views on when girls should begin
dating boys. She offered Jamie the option of meeting boys at

school or church functions and even suggested a party at their house. She carefully explained her preference that Jamie wait until she was older before dating. Even though Jamie voiced her objections, Mom did not try to force the girl to see things as she did.

Anger is not as likely to destroy family relations when it is dealt with openly and honestly. When a parent feels upset, the issue should be brought to the discussion table as soon as possible. The teen's own feelings should be acknowledged and accepted as valid. The parent should make decisions on what action will be taken to correct an imbalanced situation. The teenager must then be allowed to come to his own conclusions about how he will handle his anger in the future. When parents deal with this touchy emotion effectively, the teenager has a positive role model to follow.

---◆---

CHAPTER TWENTY-ONE

Nothing's More Important Than You!

PARENT-CHILD UNITY CAN DIMINISH ANGER

Agroup of mothers was talking about their teenaged children's hectic lifestyles. "I have a hard time knowing where my daughter is supposed to go next. You won't believe this, but we have two different calendars in our kitchen. We post all of our family plans on one calendar and use the other to keep track of Donna's activities. Guess which calendar is the more full?"

Another mother laughed with her friend and said that things were the same at her house. "My son won't be sixteen until next summer. Since he can't drive yet, he wants me to take him every-where. And I do mean *everywhere*. At least half of our arguments have something to do with his schedule. I think he wants to do too much and he accuses me of holding him back from his friends. He's constantly reminding me that there's more to being a teenager than just spending time with his family."

Her comments triggered the thoughts of a third mom. "I try to tell my daughter that I love her and want to spend time with her. That's why I keep her home sometimes. But if she feels forced to spend time with the family, you'd think I was trying to make her drink hemlock. She acts as if the whole family is poisonous!"

The mothers were comforted to know they were not alone in their concerns about their adolescent children. All had a common desire to be close to their children. Simultaneously, all felt frustrated by their teenagers' reluctance to fit the family into their schedules.

I was reminded of this group conversation a few days later when several troubled teenagers talked freely with one another about their relationships with their parents. Their remarks presented a different picture from the one painted by the group of mothers.

Said one sixteen-year-old boy, "I'll come in when it's time to eat and when I pass through the living room where my dad's sitting, he *might* grunt as I walk past him. If he says anything it's usually something like, 'Hey, get outta my way. Can't you see I'm watching the news?'" The other teens in the group laughed at their friend. He continued. "And then I'll go in the kitchen where my mother is and she says, 'Don't just stand there. Go set the table if you expect me to feed you!'"

A fifteen-year-old girl related one of her experiences. "I used to tell my parents where I was going when I went out, but I learned that only stupid people do that. The more your parents know about what you're doing, the more likely they are to tell you why you shouldn't do it! If my parents try to get me to talk to them, I give them the shortest answer I can think of. 'I don't know' usually works pretty well. It drives them nuts not knowing what I'm up to, but the way I figure it, it's their own fault. They blew it when I was willing to talk to them. Now I don't want to talk."

Another girl gave a more poignant viewpoint. "My mom tells me that if I need to talk to her I should just say so and she'll make time for me. I want to, but I'm never sure when to tell her I'm ready to talk. She just got remarried a few months ago and spends all her time with her new husband. I guess he's a nice enough guy, but he gets in the way of me and my mom. I wish she'd give me the time she gives him."

Something doesn't add up when you take the mothers' conversation and compare it to the teenagers' conversation. The parents state that their children have no time for quality family activities. Conversely, the young people suggest they would like more quality time with their parents, but feel unable to gain access to their busy or disinterested mothers and fathers.

Take the Lead in Spending Time with Your Teen

Invariably, when I meet with families of troubled teenagers, the comment will be made that too much family time is spent in arguments. Opportunities for constructive communication are somehow lost. Many parents dislike the way their relationship with their young person has evolved over the years. No adult enters parenthood intending to let their relationship with their child dwindle to nothing. Somehow, though, it can happen, even in the best of families.

Parents sometimes find themselves thrust into the unwanted role of family policeman. It is natural that the parent would search to somehow get out of that unpleasant role. They may try several tactics, including:

- using punishment to push an ungrateful teen into cooperation
- giving in and accepting the inevitable fate that the parent-child relationship will only get worse
- plea bargaining with their child in hopes of coercing the young person into remaining in the family fold
- appealing to the teenager by giving him excessive material items
- reasoning with the teen to be a greater part of the family
- comparing him to other young people who are different from him

In turn, teenagers react to parents with their own defensive maneuvers. These include:

- retaliating against parental force by putting on a display of strength and power
- emotionally detaching from their parents with the belief that it is their only hope for inner peace

- striking deals with parents with the hope of gaining a sense of control over the family
- accepting material gifts with little thanks, or even with a demand for more
- rejecting parental appeals to reason with the argument that they do not intend to be "just like" everyone else

Both angry teens and their parents will readily agree that a better way of family life must exist. When I counsel families who are groping for happiness, family members often ask *who* must take that first step toward family healing—the rebellious teen or the victimized parent? I encourage parents to take the first step in rebuilding damaged relationships.

When I mentioned this idea to one particularly proud father, he indignantly replied, "How can you suggest that I be the one to be the peacemaker in our home when my son is the one doing all the damage to our family?" For a moment I remained silent. He spoke up again before I could respond. "I suppose you're going to tell me I'm the leader of the home and it's my fatherly duty."

"You're the leader of the home," I responded. "There's not much way around it. Kenneth looks to you before deciding what his next move should be. He would probably be surprised to see you change leadership styles."

A slight smile came across this toughened father's face. "I'd kind of like to see that. Not many teenagers have heart attacks, but he probably would if his old man became softer." Silently, I smiled with this father, knowing that he had just concluded that for his son to change, he needed to lead the way.

Learn What Works When Talking to Your Teen

There is a right way and a wrong way to do virtually anything. That statement can certainly be made about the way parents approach a teenager with the intent of spending quality time with the young person. If parents are to lead in rebuilding relationships with an angry teenager, they need to know some guidelines.

There are *many* correct ways to build a healthy rapport with an adolescent. After years of talking with teenagers, they have taught me several ways to rebuild hurt family relationships. Below are some ideas teenagers offer when asked what they like to see happen when they talk with parents:

Give your undivided attention. A mother told me that she used to believe that paying attention to a teenager was simple. "You merely sit back, relax, and soak up everything the young person says." Sometimes that approach works, she stated, but at times the teenager becomes suspicious. Her son once commented, "Hey, you're *so* relaxed, I'm not sure what you're up to! Do you have something up your sleeve?" He believed she was not paying attention. Teenagers want to know that parents are truly interested in their world. As they talk, it helps to ask about his interests. Ask about the music on the radio, or comment on the teen's activities, or offer him the chance to make a decision for the family.

The adolescent must believe that the parent is willing to momentarily step into his world. This same mother later commented, "Once I learned to listen to my son, and I mean *really* listen, things began to improve at our house."

Refrain from judgmental comments. A fourteen-year-old boy told me about an uncomfortable conversation he had with his mother. "She came into my room and sat down in this 'director's chair' that I have. Her first comment was 'This thing's uncomfortable. Why would anybody want one of these?' I tried to laugh, but then she made a couple of comments about how my room would look better if we rearranged it and how she couldn't stand the music playing on the stereo. After a few minutes, I didn't want to laugh, even though she said she was just kidding." When I asked how he responded to his mother's comments, he replied, "I just got quiet and said nothing. She finally left That was three weeks ago and she hasn't been in my room since then"

This young man initially liked it when his mother wandered into his room to spend a few minutes in casual conversation. Instead of capitalizing on her son's desire to spend time with her, the brief conversation ended in silence when the boy heard little more than unwanted advice and opinions.

Show your teen you understand. As we have learned, parents may not show understanding for fear of conveying agreement. It seems risky to say to a teenaged daughter, "It seems that so many of your friends are sexually active. It makes you wonder if something's wrong with you because you're not." It feels odd to react to an upset son by saying, "When Mr. Henderson gave you three days in detention hall for talking back to Mrs. Lindley, you felt like telling him that Mrs. Lindley is just as guilty as you and should also have to stay after school."

Try to imagine the look on your teenager's face if you made a statement like those above. Your teen may be surprised that your thoughts paralleled his. Yet, your child will feel a sense of relief that silently says, *It sure feels good to know that my mom knows exactly what I'm feeling right now.*

Be assured that your child can accurately state your views on premarital sex, or defiance of authority figures, or other potentially explosive issues. Your teen will not believe you have suddenly made an about-face in your stance on important family and social matters. He will simply view you as an understanding adult.

Teenagers who feel understood by parents often move to a deeper level of communication. She may say, "I do have a lot of questions about what's right and what's wrong about sex." Or, he may say, "Sometimes I wish I had the chance to change the rules at my school. I'd do things differently."

A teenager who knows that his parents understand his viewpoint is far more receptive when he receives sound parental advice. Understanding responses lead the teen to deeper levels of thought. The understanding parent is one the adolescent trusts for guidance.

Keep personal matters confidential. One day I had back to back appointments with two teenage boys. One teen felt that his relationship with his parents was on the rebound. He told me that he did not feel the same urge to angrily blast his parents that he felt only weeks earlier. He stated, "I can tell my dad things and know it will stay between me and him." He talked of how good it felt that his father had made adjustments in their communication.

The very next hour, I listened as another teenager talked of how he would never again trust his thoughts to his father. He said, "When I told my father about a problem I was having with my girlfriend, I thought he knew I didn't want him telling anyone else. But when I went to school a couple days later, this guy comes up to me and starts kidding me about this deal with my girlfriend. Know how he found out about it? My dad had talked to his dad, and his dad couldn't keep his mouth shut. Now the whole world knows my business." This teenager spent his time talking with me about his wounded sense of trust.

Most teenagers consider it dangerous to reveal their real feelings to others. Notice how often one youth will gain a pledge from another to keep matters private before revealing a secret. ("You promise you won't tell?") Teenagers rightly assume that mothers and fathers will keep personal matters to themselves. Failing to do so is a sure bet to break the ties that bind families together.

Help the teen draw conclusions. One disadvantage of being a parent who wants to help a teenaged child is that we were all once teenagers ourselves. Let me explain that seemingly contradictory comment.

Experience is the harshest, but surest, teacher of life's truths. Teenagers are at a point in development in which they have similar intellectual abilities as their parents. Between the ages of eleven and fourteen adult-like mental capacity emerges in young people. Intellectual capacity is virtually complete by the time a young person reaches the age of seventeen years. At that age teenagers are capable of reasoning, from a purely intellectual standpoint, with adults. The major difference between teens and adults is that adults necessarily have much more experience in life than teenagers. I might add that this difference is a big one!

It is only through life experiences that practical judgment, common sense, and wisdom are groomed. Nothing else can replace time for the development of these mental abilities. If you want an interesting conversation, though, try to convince a teenager of this truth! Youthful naivete deceives many teens into believing that they understand far more than their limited experiences have taught them.

Parents face a major disadvantage in coping with inexperienced teenagers. Because parents are on the "other side" of life, it is difficult to remember how teens think. Life has taught parents many harsh realities about life and relationships. We now see things differently than when we were young. Because once-clouded truths are now crystal clear in our adult eyes, we cannot recall the near-sighted vision of our own youth. Think of the last time you attempted to convince your teen to see things your way. Recall your exasperation at your child's inability to grasp your simple logic. Understanding takes time. It did for you. It will for your child, too.

Guiding a teenager through life's experiences is an art form. An understanding parent can be a companion to a teen when tough decisions must be made—decisions such as which peers to associate with, or whether or not to experiment with alcohol or drugs, or where religious concepts fit in his life, or how to handle sexual pressures. But the teenager is ultimately responsible for the choices he makes. The parent is simply a guide. The teen who feels no parental understanding has limited choices about how important decisions will be made. He can listen to other (inexperienced) youth, blindly choose and hope for the best, or pray that some other significant adult comes along to show him the way to happiness.

A parent often is the best counselor an angry teen can have.

Most people assume that counselors are supposed to offer a lot of advice. This is true to a degree. The most vital role of the counselor, though, is to listen, show the young person understanding, offer evidence of his personal value, and help clarify confusing thoughts and emotions. Parents who step into that role in the home help diffuse an adolescent's anger. Watching the child grow into healthy behavior and relationships is only a by-product of those efforts.

CHAPTER TWENTY-TWO

◆——

I Forgive You

ANGER CONTROL INVOLVES FORGIVENESS

Forgiveness is a word that gets tossed around a lot. We all realize that forgiveness is required to heal broken relationships. Forgiveness is a word that we assume all people can define. It simply means letting bygones be bygones, right? Well, it sort of means that, but it also means much more. Forgiveness is a deceptively complex concept. Angry teenagers hear this word just like the rest of us, but many do not fully comprehend its depth or potential healing power.

CASE STUDY: *Jesse Sneaks Out*

Fourteen-year-old Jesse was so angry he was near the point of tears. His face was streaked with an intensity suggesting that something awful was happening inside him. His face was red and his blood pressure was surely on the rise. He had just told me how furious he was with his mother and father over an incident that had happened several nights earlier.

Jesse had sneaked out of his house to meet a group of friends at a rendezvous point down the street. One of the older boys in the group was to slip away in his father's car and pick up Jesse and two other boys at midnight. The plan had apparently unfolded without a hitch. The driver arrived precisely when he said he would. The group of adolescents spent a carefree night at a bowling alley where they rented a lane until three o'clock that morning. Their activity completed, each boy assumed that sneaking back into their respective houses would be a simple matter.

To the dismay of the foursome, each was greeted by their parents who had discovered their sons' absence. It seems that the driver's father heard his son pushing his car down the street and alerted the parents of his three best friends, whom he correctly guessed would be in on the late night excursion.

Jesse continued to seethe anger as he told the rest of the story. "My parents got bent out of shape a whole lot worse than my friends' parents. I admit it, I got caught. I shouldn't have snuck out of the house, but I did and there's nothing I can do to change it. I said I was sorry, but that wasn't good enough. They'll probably ground me until I leave home for college. I think my parents want me to beg them to forgive me. I can't do that. All I can do is say I'm sorry and hope that they will accept my apology."

"And that's what's got you so upset. You've admitted to your parents your mistake, but it seems that's not good enough."

"What else can I do?" Jesse shot back. "I can't predict the future. They want me to promise I won't do anything like I did last weekend ever again. How can I make that promise? I can guarantee you I'm going to make more mistakes. It's like I'm in a no-win situation. If I tell them I won't ever mess up again, they'll call me a liar when I do. If I say there's no way I can promise not to make another mistake, they'll accuse me of having a bad attitude!"

Trying to think as Jesse was thinking, I commented, "If we had to ask your parents right now if your attitude was bad, they would probably say it is. They know you're angry, and they assume that your anger means you don't care about their rules."

Jesse let loose with even stronger emotion, "Well, they're right. I *am* angry! And unless they give me half a chance, I probably *will* do it again—just to show them how bad I can be!"

Jesse's parents presented a different side of the story. "We were very disappointed with Jesse when he sneaked out of the house the other night," explained his mother. "Those boys he was with are all basically good kids. I know they were just out to have fun, but they simply failed to stop and think of what kind of trouble they could have gotten into. I can't think of much good that happens at bowling alleys between midnight and three o'clock in the morning."

Her husband added his thoughts. "I tried to tell Jesse that he could have been hurt, but he wouldn't listen. All he wanted to focus on was that he and his friends weren't drinking or driving wild or breaking any laws. We felt forced to punish him harshly just so he would get the message that we don't want him to do the same thing again."

Here we have a case in which a young adolescent has acted unwisely. He saw it as normal teenage mischief. His parents saw it as potentially dangerous. After the incident had passed, Jesse was left with more anger than he had before he disobeyed his parents' rules. His parents were more strongly gripped by fear for their child's safety.

Forgiveness Bypasses Revenge

Many angry teenagers complain that their parents want to "get back" at them for making a mistake. Jesse believed that about his parents. However, most parents do not punish simply to emotionally level their child. Punishment is given in order to teach the youth to be more careful in future decision making. That is what Jesse's parents had in mind. It is important, though, to take seriously the teen's reaction to punishment. After all, the teenager's interpretation of the punishment will determine its effectiveness in preventing future mistakes. In front of his parents, I asked Jesse to elaborate on how he felt "put down" by his parents' reaction to the "bowling alley incident." Here are some of the things he named:

- *As soon as I walked in the door, I knew I was in big trouble because both of them had a really angry look on their faces.*

- *They didn't even give me a chance to talk when I came in the house. Both of them started asking me a million questions about where I had been and what I was doing.*
- *They assumed I had been drinking and wouldn't believe me until my friends' parents convinced them.*
- *When I tried to explain why I had done what I did, I didn't get a chance to finish what I wanted to say.*
- *They punished me too hard.*

After Jesse had completed his comments, I said, "I don't imagine that's what your parents wanted you to dwell on." Jesse's parents shook their heads in agreement. "I would guess that they did what they did because they were worried about you and don't want you to make poor judgments again." After a brief pause, I looked at Jesse, "But that's not the message you got, is it?" Jesse indicated it was not. I continued, "In fact, I'm afraid you feel even more rebellious now than ever." Jesse would not look up. His silence indicated just how angry he was.

The act of forgiveness begins *before* a young person makes a mistake. Forgiveness of a teenager starts when parents maintain the kind of detachment from the teenager's mistakes that allows for a controlled emotional response. To become entangled in the youth's blunders sends a message: *Your problem has become my problem and I'm going to force a solution to it.* Remaining emotionally detached from adolescent errors sends a different message: *You have the responsibility for solving the problems you create. I have enough interest in you, though, that I plan to help out.*

Probably the most famous example of parental forgiveness is the well-known biblical story of the Prodigal Son. In this familiar parable, a son makes a reckless and impulsive decision to take his inheritance at an early age so he can spend it living as he wishes. For a short while he lives the good life, but once his riches are spent, the good life suddenly disappears. Mired in depression and shame, he returns home to his father with the hope of regaining at least some semblance of a decent lifestyle. The welcome he receives from his father far exceeds what he expected. Instead of chastisement, humiliation, punishment, or scorn, Father welcomes his son with open arms—a parent who had waited patiently for his boy's return.

Of the many lessons gleaned from this parable, one that stands out is that true forgiveness is offered without having to be asked for. No strings are attached. We are told that the father saw the boy from a distance and ran to greet him. This suggests that the parent had decided to separate his feelings about his son from his feelings about his son's behavior. There is little doubt that the Prodigal knew that his father's forgiveness did not mean he condoned the mistakes. The decision to forgive was based on the father's desire to replenish an empty relationship, nothing else. It was made well in advance of the youth's eventual return home. We can correctly assume that the father disagreed with the youth's poor choices, but this did not affect his choice to be forgiving.

I used the example of the Prodigal Son once in a talk dealing with parental forgiveness. Afterward, a questioning mother asked, "But don't you think it would be wrong to simply forgive and forget and let your child know that there will be no consequences for his actions?"

My response was, "Yes, I do."

"Well, then, the story about the Prodigal Son gives the wrong impression because that's what seems to have happened. The boy got off scot-free. Nothing happened to him to teach him right from wrong!"

There are times we are so intent on knowing all the many details of a story that we lose sight of its major points. My guess would be that if this famous story were carried further, we would find that the father's future management of his son would take into account the boy's history of irresponsibility. Perhaps he would be given greater supervision, or would have no more opportunity to partake of the family's wealth, or would be required to make amends for any damages incurred.

To dwell on what happens after forgiveness is given can cause us to miss the point of the story entirely, though. Forgiveness is an act that focuses on bringing healing to wounded relationships.

But What about the Next Mistake?

Try as we may to focus our energies on the healing aspects of forgiveness, we are still stuck with the question of what to do when the young person makes yet another mistake. Is a parent to keep on forgiving over and over? The answer is a resounding "Yes!" Forgiveness is not an action as much as it is a personal characteristic. It is a quality that should characterize all family relationships, regardless of how often it must be shown.

Most teenagers drool when I tell parents that I believe that a young person should be allowed as much flexibility as he can responsibly handle. The only part of that phrase the teenager usually hears is the word "flexibility" and little of the rest. Somehow the idea of "responsibility" gets lost in the shuffle. I've even had a few parents question my judgment, or sanity, or both when I have uttered that statement.

I like to recommend keeping behavior management decisions separate from the act of forgiveness. Let me further explain. To display forgiveness means that the relationship between parent and child is given top priority. The parent tries to avoid those communication barriers that block family growth. Forgiveness is conveyed through:

- displaying an even tone of voice
- showing emotional control
- quickly returning to a normal routine
- refraining from judgmental comments
- keeping critical remarks brief
- sticking to the situation at hand
- avoiding references to past errors

To forgive a young person is to emphasize his obvious need to be reaffirmed. The very fact that the teen needs to be forgiven indicates that a mistake has been made. To dwell on a lapse in judgment without also addressing the need for encouragement typically leaves the youth feeling empty—and angry.

Wisdom dictates that while the forgiving parent works to rebuild a bruised parent-child bond, adjustments in family management must also be made. The parent must keep in mind that the chances are strong that the teenager will disagree with the parent's disciplinary decisions. Knowing in advance of the teenager's disagreement somehow helps the parent feel less offended by the inevitable verbal retaliation.

The following offers an example of how parental forgiveness and disciplinary decisions can be effectively intertwined.

SITUATION: Jerri's mother caught her in a lie. She had told her mother she would be at her next door neighbor's house when in fact she met a group of boys down the street. Jerri's mother feels betrayed when she sees her daughter with these beer-drinking and cigarette-smoking boys. She decides she needs to confront her daughter's deceit.

PARENTAL REACTION: Mother calls Jerri home. When the daughter comes sulking into the house, Mother quietly tells her it is time to eat supper. Jerri does not eat much during mealtime. She tries to engage her mother in an argument by offering excuses for slipping down the street. Mother refrains from being drawn into a war of words with her daughter.

The next time Jerri announces her intentions to go out, Mother agrees, but only after verifying her daughter's plans. Jerri is miffed that her mother doesn't trust her, but gives in to the fact that her mother will supervise her more closely than before. Mother makes a point to spend extra time with Jerri over the next few days. During these conversations, little is said about

Jerri's mistake. Instead, mother and daughter talk about other things.

ANALYSIS: Mother sent a continual message of forgiveness by refusing to be drawn into squabbles that would only further harm their relationship. The emotional control she showed suggested that she loved Jerri too much to cut loose with unbridled anger and frustration. She made necessary adjustments in managing Jerri's behavior when she verified Jerri's future plans. A second time, she stayed away from another potential argument, but refused to be negotiable when Jerri had just shown she could not handle flexibility. She continued to show a forgiving attitude when she found extra time to talk with her daughter. Her refusal to hold a grudge against Jerri sent the tacit message that past mistakes would not become a barrier to their relationship.

Psychologists often talk about the parent's need to offer logical consequences to a misbehaving young person. I agree that the parent's response should match the child's responsibility. Too often, though, behavioral consequences are given in an unforgiving spirit. Along with making behavioral adjustments parents may:

- argue with the teen
- try to force unnecessary confessions from the teen
- bring up past mistakes
- make accusations or call names
- make comparisons to other teenagers
- offer negative predictions about the future

To discipline with a judgmental spirit erases the chance for the teen to feel forgiven. Forgiveness removes barriers that hurt family relations. A forgiven teenager can more readily forgive himself for the mistakes he has made. He can more easily accept responsibility for the choices he has made. He can eventually learn to see himself, faults and all, more objectively. Forgiveness clears the way for healthier communication between parent and child. Forgiveness gives the teen a good reason to keep anger in its right place.

◆

CHAPTER TWENTY-THREE

Set the Rules Straight

HEALTHY EMOTIONAL EXCHANGE REQUIRES BOUNDARIES

Have you ever noticed how much angry teenagers grumble and complain? Of course, any adolescent with intense emotions will do his fair share of fussing. One sure thing that starts anger on its destructive course is a gnawing feeling of dissatisfaction. An angry teenager does not want to accept things as they are. At times, his dissatisfaction is warranted, but at other times it is poorly founded. Young people voice their complaints in numerous ways. Here are some of the more common complaints of a dissatisfied teen:

- *Nobody around here ever tells me I'm important.*
- *I don't have a voice in what happens to me.*
- *The rules around here are stupid and old-fashioned.*
- *My parents say they will do one thing and then they do something different.*
- *I feel lonely even when other people are around.*
- *Sometimes I truly don't care what happens to me.*
- *I wish I could run away and start my life all over.*
- *It seems that nothing I do helps anymore.*
- *I honestly question whether my family loves me.*

If you spend any time around teenagers it quickly becomes evident that they not only tell others how they feel, they also show it in their behavior. It is the negative behavior teenagers display that attracts so much attention from adults. Just think of how often you have had to ground your teenager, or take away a prized privilege, or step in and break up a fight. More than one parent has said to me, "It seems that all I ever do is punish my teenager. He doesn't like it, and it certainly doesn't give me the jollies either!"

You've no doubt heard this next statement before, but I'm going to give it to you one more time: *The most effective kind of discipline is preventative discipline.* As simplistic as that statement seems, engaging in preventative discipline is actually quite complex. To effectively do so requires a well thought-out plan. Consistency in sticking to the plan is a must. Following are some of the most important elements of helping your teenager effectively manage his anger. When used in combination with well-placed communication, the net result can be a decrease in the teen's anger.

Pay Your Teenager Regularly

No doubt that heading got your attention. It's a serious recommendation. Think for a moment of how your job would be if you were issued a paycheck only when your boss was in the mood to give you one. And whenever he did give you a paycheck, he arbitrarily decided how much money should be enclosed. And you were never sure if the check would bounce whenever you tried to cash it in at the bank. You would be one unhappy worker, would you not? In fact, you would probably be angry! After all, you would depend on that paycheck to pay for your various needs. If it happened routinely, do you think you would quit that job and look for another? Probably so. I would.

Teenagers are no different from adults when it comes to the need to be paid accurately and consistently. Just as an employee needs to be rewarded for doing his job, teenagers need a reward for doing whatever it is teenagers are expected to do. Look at the expectations you have for your adolescent child as a kind of job description. When you tell your child what is expected and what is disallowed, you are, in essence, doing the same thing an employer does with his employees. And just as the employee needs to be rewarded with a paycheck and other kinds of recognition, so too does the young person.

When I say to pay your teenager, I do not mean you have to *literally* offer your child money for every single job he performs. Payment can take many shapes and forms. Consider these easy ways you can "pay" a teenager for doing anything you consider to be positive:

- take out the trash for him on trash day (with him holding the door for you)
- make a favorite dessert as a way of saying "thanks" for trying
- let him decide what you will fix for dinner tonight
- allow him to use your favorite baseball glove at his next game
- squeeze her shoulders as you brag on her in front of some friends
- agree to turn the radio up loud—just this once—as you cruise down the road
- edge the driveway while he mows the lawn
- write down the answers to her homework as she dictates
- wear whatever she picks out the next time you take her somewhere
- turn all the air conditioning vents in his direction as you drive in your hot car

Notice that it does not have to cost you a nickel to "pay" your teenager. By sending a positive message to your child, you are simply saying, "Thank you for doing your job." It is the adolescent's job to grow into responsibility. One of the parent's jobs is to give the kinds of responses that let the young person know he is appreciated for his efforts. A well-paid teenager finds it easy to shed unneeded anger.

Run from Potential Fights

There will inevitably be times when your teenager will need a negative consequence. As discussed in the previous chapter, it is a fact of family life that all adolescents will make mistakes. As I talk with parents, it is readily apparent that the most unenjoyable part of parenting involves punishment. None of us like to do it. Teenagers are fully aware of this fact and are willing to exploit it!

A conversation I had with a father typifies the feelings of many other parents. He explained that his son had violated a minor household rule. The young man had worn his brother's shirt without first asking permission from his sibling. "I simply told Lonnie to tell his brother he was sorry and to wash it with a load of his own clothes before he put it back in his brother's closet. You would have thought I had taken a stick and beaten him if you had seen his reaction!"

"I take that to mean he didn't respond too favorably to the consequence you gave him for breaking a rule," I said in an understatement.

The father continued. "He proceeded to tell me that he shouldn't have to wash the shirt because his brother had worn it earlier in the week. He said his brother would have washed it anyway, so he didn't see why I was punishing him in that way."

"So what happened next?"

"It just went downhill from there. I tried to make him wash it, and he got stubborn and refused to cooperate. Then I told him if that was his attitude, he was grounded for a week. He didn't like that because he had plans for the weekend. When I told him he had to cancel them, he became furious and ranted and raved at how unfair I was being. I told him he was the one being unfair to his brother. When he wouldn't stop yapping, I took away his phone privileges for the week too. It ended up that he stayed holed up in his room for most of the next two days and would hardly speak to the family for several days, except to complain. Just think, all of that started when I simply asked him to wash a shirt that he shouldn't have been wearing in the first place."

To understand how to effectively place boundaries around an angry teenager, I like to step into the young person's world and view the situation through his eyes. Using the illustration involving Lonnie and his father as an example, notice how Lonnie's thoughts progressed as he pushed the limits of his father's emotional tolerance.

- Lonnie expressed his displeasure with his father's request to apologize to his brother and wash the shirt in his next load of laundry.
- Lonnie refused to acknowledge that it was only logical to wash his brother's shirt before returning it. Seeing that Dad would try to punish him into compliance, Lonnie knew the fight for control was on.
- Lonnie successfully punished Dad by frustrating him with a display of rebellion and disrespect.
- Lonnie continued to control the tempo of the home as he sulked for several days, refusing to communicate pleasantly with the family.

Lonnie learned that the emotional boundaries in his home were moveable. Through the course of time he had discovered that if he could raise the emotional intensity of the family, he could possibly change the rules of the house. Like other young people, he had learned that his aggression would make his parents think twice the next time they thought about confronting him. Even if he received extra punishment for his bad attitude, he could take pleasure in knowing that his anger was potent enough to control the atmosphere of the home. Even though he was upset, he could take delight in knowing that the rest of the family was upset, too. Unfortunately, he would simultaneously see his own anger grow out of control.

To keep Lonnie's anger from getting out of hand, the father

would have done well to refrain from Lonnie's invitation to fight. Having stated the boundary (apologize to your brother and wash his shirt), Lonnie's verbal protest should be ignored. The parent's obligation to the child is to follow up to ensure that the stated job is carried out. An uncooperative teen response would signal the parent to make unpopular choices later on when the young person wants a favor or privilege. But, *all parental responses must be emotionally controlled*. As the young person sees that arguing receives a neutral response and does not change the rules or the emotional state of the family, the youth can more easily dowse his own anger. What's more, the added commotion that accompanies undesirable arguments will be avoided.

Use Punishment Carefully

A quick word about punishment should accompany any discussion about helping a young person get his anger under control: *Punishment is not an effective behavior management tool if overused or used in the absence of frequent rewards*. I am often asked to name as many creative punishments as I can think of to erase a teenager's anger. Try as I may, I have yet to find a magical weapon that will purge a teenager of his anger. I can look for the rest of my life and I still will not discover the secret punishment for teenage behavior problems. It simply does not exist.

I had two separate conversations with parents who were concerned about their child's growing problem with angry outbursts. The first parent detailed all of her daughter's negative behaviors. She gave a long checklist of punishments she had used to squelch her teen's rebellion. The list included grounding her, taking away a multitude of privileges, isolating her from her friends, refusing to talk to her, and taking away her allowance. With an exasperated voice she sighed, "And nothing has worked. Do you have any better suggestions?"

The conversation with the second parent began in a similar fashion. "My son has been insistent on breaking every rule he can think of. My initial reaction was to pull out all the stops and punish him so hard that he would think twice before doing something foolish again. It hit me like a ton of bricks after several days of nonstop fighting that my punishments were only making things worse instead of better. I realized I hadn't said a kind word to him for days. It was no wonder he didn't want to cooperate with me. Why should he? I was being an old hag. I quit trying to punish my son into submission and when he saw me change my approach to him, he suddenly became more cooperative."

The insight of this second mother can be applied to all families. No young person enjoys constant conflict. Listen to these comments from frequently punished teens.

- *I'd give anything if my family wouldn't argue and fight all the time.*
- *I wish my parents wouldn't punish me to try to make me do what they want. It doesn't work.*
- *When I see a friend getting along well with his parents, it gives me a sick feeling inside.*
- *The only time my parents talk to me is to tell me how long I'm grounded. I hate that.*
- *I've wanted to tell my parents what I feel, but if I did I'd get in trouble.*
- *When I get punished, all I can think about is how to get back at my parents.*

Though it may be hard to believe, teenagers do not like conflict any more than the rest of the family. Their comments, though, suggest that when parents try to force change with regular punishment, it tends to fuel the flames of anger rather than extinguish them.

There is a term used by psychologists that explains what happens when punishment only makes matters worse in a family. That term is *negative reinforcement*. Simply put, negative reinforcement is a response that causes an *increase* in a negative behavior. The parent may view her response to a teenager as a punishment, hoping that the negative behavior will decrease, but the teenager may see it differently. Consider the following examples.

SITUATION: Jeff made a low grade in his biology class because of lax study habits. His parents punish him by taking away his telephone privileges until his grades improve.

TEEN'S REACTION: Jeff feels like giving up on himself. While sitting alone in his room, he mutters "I can't do anything right." He loses interest in biology and makes an even lower grade on his next report card.

ANALYSIS: Although his parents intended to motivate Jeff to do better in school, their punishment *reinforced* his feelings of inadequacy. His self-confidence shaken, he gave up in his biology class.

SITUATION: Hearing Sheila and her younger sister, Valerie, arguing with one another, Mother went to see what all the fuss was about. Valerie complained that Sheila refused to clean her part of their bedroom. Sheila claimed that the items strewn on the floor were Valerie's. Not wanting to hear their bickering, Mother screamed, "Stop it! Both of you clean up this room. Sheila, you can't go out tonight. You're grounded for arguing."

TEEN'S REACTION: Feeling unjustly punished, Sheila only halfheartedly did as her mother demanded. Furious that her sister caused her to be grounded, she made numerous snide remarks to Valerie that night to show her contempt. The anger swelled inside her.

ANALYSIS: Sheila viewed her punishment as evidence that Mother did not understand what had really happened. The quick pronouncement of a penalty convinced the teen to take justice into her own hands. Instead of squelching her rebellious feelings, the punishment *increased* their intensity.

When using punishment to contain teenage anger, the following considerations should be kept in mind.

- Make use of the lightest punishment needed to get your message across. Remember, your aim is to react in a way that will decrease the likelihood of further negative behavior. Punishment does not need to be administered with a sledgehammer to be effective.
- Constantly view your response as your teenager would view it. What may seem like a punishment to you may be interpreted differently by your child. Learn to think the way your teenager thinks.
- Let the punishment stand on its own. It is common to administer punishment with an accompanying lecture, sermon, or dramatic display of emotions. It is these accompanying gestures and statements that usually cause your teenager to misinterpret your intended message.
- After administering a punishment, wait until your teen's anger has subsided and then give him the chance to express his feelings. Listen carefully without becoming defensive. Try to show that while you may disagree with him, you are able to understand him.
- Remember that constructive criticism or punishment is most effective when it comes from an adult who has a good rapport with the teenager. The time you spend building a positive relationship with your teen will pay off when you must step into the role of authority figure.
- Make sparing use of punishment. Make much more frequent use of positive comments and reactions. Try to keep a ratio of

at least three to one in favor of positive responses. To see how you are doing in following this guideline, keep score on yourself. Slipping into a punitive habit of reacting to teenagers is easier than we would like to admit.

◆

CHAPTER TWENTY-FOUR

A Lesson on Climate Control

THE HOME ATMOSPHERE AND ANGER RESOLUTION

My wife and children tease me for my interest in the weather. Many evenings my wife, Julie, will ask me as I sit in our den watching the latest news about weather conditions, "What are you watching, Lee?"

Knowing full well that I am being set up, I give my usual brief response. "The weather."

I cringe as Julie announces my personal business to the rest of the family. "Girls! Be quiet! Dad's watching the weather. We don't want him to miss it. Don't come in here and bother him for the next couple hours until he's got tomorrow's forecast completely memorized!"

Of course, Julie's broadcast is effective. It draws our three daughters to the den so they can join their gloating mother. The four of them stare at me in mock amazement as I try to enlighten myself about the next day's weather.

"Something wrong with all of you?" I might ask.

"Don't mind us, Dad," one the girls will say. "We just didn't know it was so hard to memorize the weather forecast."

"Hmpf. Just don't ask me tomorrow if you should wear a sweater or a short-sleeved shirt. And if you get caught in the rain, don't expect to get under my umbrella because you can't." Somehow, my remarks have no impact on my family. Julie and the girls refuse to take me seriously.

Know Your Home's Condition

Despite how my family harasses me about my interest in the weather, I like to know what to expect from our world. It helps to know if it will be warm, rainy, foggy, windy, or any combination of these conditions over the next few days. Just as I (and many others, thank you) like to keep track of atmospheric conditions, the family should keep an eye on the emotional barometer of the home.

You have probably been in a home where all is chaos. The house is cluttered, the activity level is a bit too brisk, everyone's voice is at full volume, and the emotional intensity is revved up high. You have also been in homes in which there is a pleasant sense of order, family members talk in a calm tone of voice, activities are well-choreographed, and cooperation is an operative word.

Families can take an inventory of the atmospheric conditions of the home to identify ways to control potentially harmful emotional exchanges. When parents try to ease teenagers from an angry pose to one that is more relaxed, not enough attention is given to these intangible circumstances. More often, attention is given to how the angry teen should be disciplined or how to talk to the disgruntled youth. These factors are certainly important and have been given proper consideration as we have dealt with teenage anger throughout this book. To give the teenager the treatment needed to get a grip on anger, though, it is vital to be aware of the positive effects of a healthy home environment.

Be Your Family's Weather Expert

Examine with me an outline of what I consider to be the most important elements of a calming home atmosphere. Maybe we could call it a forecast for a healthy home environment.

Keep the house warm. A teenage girl told of a time when she approached her father as he sat in his bedroom reading a book. "I walked into the bedroom and began telling my dad about this science project I was doing for school. I asked Dad if he had a minute to talk. I didn't want him to help me with the assignment. I just wanted him to tell me if he thought it was a good idea. He said, 'Sure,' so I began telling him what I had in mind. As I was talking, he kept looking down at the book he was reading. I know he wasn't listening to me. I finally said, 'Never mind' and left the room. You know what really bugs me about the whole thing? I think my dad was hardly aware that I had walked out."

Emotional warmth is not something that is communicated through words as much as through behavior. The display of warmth is a nonverbal way to tell a teenager "I love you." Households need to keep the emotional thermostat turned up so the teenager knows she is important. Warmth is shown in a variety of ways including:

- paying attention when the child is communicating
- making positive gestures through eye contact
- wearing a pleasant facial expression
- expressing interest through the tone of voice used
- touching the young person with affection
- giving attention to the teen's interests

Offering the teenager a warm atmosphere helps to dispel anger by assuring the young person of her importance to the family. Nonverbal cues that deny the teen's value to the family provide a breeding ground for unhealthy anger.

Create an experimental atmosphere. In his closing remarks to the first biblical letter to the Thessalonians, the apostle Paul counsels, "Examine everything carefully; hold fast to that which is good" (1 Thess. 5:21). Paul's advice is appropriate for the home. Many parents tend to send the message, *"Don't* examine anything; let *me* tell you what is good." Of course, this parental suggestion is usually meant to keep the inexperienced youth from unnecessary harm, but its good intentions may backfire. A world that discourages experi-

239

mentation pushes the teen to a potentially harmful curiosity about the ways of the world.

"My parents wouldn't let me do anything," expressed a rebellious college-aged teenager. "I couldn't wait to get out of the house. I had no idea what went on after eleven o'clock at night because my parents wouldn't let me out of the house. The harder I'd push for freedom, the more they would hold me back. I kept telling myself that as soon as I left for college I wouldn't live the way my parents had been forcing me to live. I wanted to find out some things on my own."

"So that explains some of the mistakes you've made," I responded to this young person who was on the verge of emotional collapse.

"I don't know. All I can say is that I don't regret one single thing I've done. I don't care how much it has hurt me. I had to find out one way or another, so I did."

Teens who are given a voice in family decisions are less likely to be swallowed up by anger. Parents who have given their children the chance to choose, even though some of those choices will certainly be wrong, have the security that their teen is capable of making decisions. Using a democratic process in the home (with the parents as leaders who allow children an important voice in decision making) helps teens and parents stay connected to one another. Teenagers are more prone to listen to warnings from parents who encourage independence.

Keep calm under fire. "I'll bet you wouldn't have told a parent sitting in your office to act like that," my teenaged daughter told me. Ouch! That comment hurt. Of course, it was intended to sting me. I had just spoken to my child in a tone of voice that left no doubt about where I stood on a certain issue. My daughter's comment indicated I had communicated more than I meant. Instead of effectively guiding her to improve her behavior, I had contributed to a negative atmosphere in our household.

A Lesson on Climate Control

It is important to look at the statements we convey silently. It is also vital to recognize the effects of a harsh tone of voice on the home atmosphere. Notice the ways a parent's tone of voice can change the home environment:

- tension will arise in a matter of seconds
- competition for control of the home may increase
- minor conflicts can swell into major battles
- family members will not seek physical or emotional closeness
- open communication will come to a screeching halt
- the teen may withhold future conciliatory gestures

Conversely, in an emotionally calm home, the following effects may be seen in the home atmosphere:

- family members will remain relaxed
- cooperation is more likely among family members
- disagreements will be settled more quickly
- physical touch will communicate greater affection
- teens will more likely reveal their inner thoughts and feelings
- adjustments in family relationships will be more readily accepted

Work together as a unit. When I first get to know different teenagers, I like them to describe their families to me. I am often surprised at how accurately teenagers will describe the thoughts and feelings of their parents and siblings. Teenagers can be quite perceptive about the inner workings of a family. One of the questions I frequently ask young people is, "How well does your family work together?" Of course, the answers I receive are as varied as the young people I talk to. Several common responses are voiced by teens who struggle to manage their anger. They include:

- *My parents don't agree on anything.*
- *If my mom won't let me do something, I go to my dad.*

- *My mother (or father) and brother (or sister) team up against me.*
- *When Mom is mad at my sister, she takes it out on me.*
- *No one in our house can agree on anything.*
- *If I can get my parents in a fight, I can get what I want.*
- *The only way I can get back at my family is to make them as mad as I am.*
- *No one in our family knows what anyone else is doing.*

In virtually any organization, be it a business, a school, a club, or a sports team, unity is one of the essential ingredients that makes that group successful. The same is true for the family. Family members should be able to sense that each member is pulling together for the good of the other. Of course, parents cannot directly control how one child will react to another, but as leaders of the home, several things can be done to encourage unity in the family. They include:

- withholding disagreeable comments until the time is right for discussion
- waiting until all the facts are in before making judgments
- viewing difficult family circumstances as other family members would view them
- publicly apologizing for mistakes or errors in judgment
- showing flexibility when the situation calls for it
- making regular time for the family to sit down and talk about both informal and serious matters

Teens always notice parental efforts to pull the family together. One teenager whose family had struggled emotionally after a particularly difficult divorce commented, "If it wasn't for the way my mom handled things, I don't know what I would have done. She kept her cool when my brother and I didn't. She brought us together a lot to talk about how we felt. She let us know that whatever had happened to her and Dad, she wasn't going to let the rest of the family fall apart." This mother's efforts to pull together a fragmented family greatly reduced the devastation of the anger that accompanied a trying divorce.

Provide spiritual leadership. Manny was one of the angriest teenagers I have seen. He was extremely bright and had experienced great success by most people's standards. Even so, he was unhappy and disgruntled. During one of our talks, he made a comment that struck at the root of his disenchantment. "Dr. Carter, do you know that even though I am seventeen years old, my parents have yet to explain to me what they believe about God or what this life is all about. I'm so lost, I have no idea where I'm going with my life."

Manny was bright enough to recognize that he was aimlessly drifting through life. Many other young people are in the same situation, only they are unaware of just how lost they are. Take note of the telltale signs of emptiness the next time you see a group of angry teens. The way the young people dress and decorate their bodies speaks loudly of their need to be noticed. Their language may show a shallowness that is only meant to impress others. There are often displays of inappropriate sexuality indicating unmet needs for affection and approval. The list could go on and on detailing the lost identity of many of today's young people.

Most parents prefer to let someone else teach their teenager about morality, ethics, or spirituality. The reason for parental inaction could possibly be the discomfort we adults feel with such issues.

I do not advocate forcing religious beliefs or moral teachings on adolescents. Teenagers rebel against almost anything that is offered with no other choice. Yet, it is equally careless to assume that teenagers will learn about the heavier side of life from some source outside the home. Following are guidelines that set a tone in the home for encouraging personal growth in the searching teenager:

- Look for opportunities to discuss "heavy" topics such as moral dilemmas or religious issues with your teenager. Doing so in a nonthreatening way helps your child look beyond the basic needs of life to those that add richness and meaning.
- Practice behavior that "preaches." For example, if you have an opportunity to be a Good Samaritan in the presence of your teen, use that situation to teach a lesson that words alone cannot adequately convey.
- When your teenager complains about a difficult personal circumstance, comment aloud on the inner struggle you think your teen must be experiencing. Help him talk out his thoughts and emotions by being an active listener.
- Take opportunities to point out matters of spiritual relevance or moral importance. Avoid, however, the urge to launch into a sermon.
- Guide your teenager to make decisions that fit your belief system. Teach your teenager that their decisions must take into account the needs of others.
- Give of yourself to others in an unselfish way. Include your teenager whenever you can. A young person who learns to give learns that the world does not spin around him.

Keep tabs on your own emotional health. A weary mother sighed as she said, "I give and give to my children, but it seems that the more I give, the worse things get. I'm tired." Before long, she and I were in a discussion of how her self-esteem had suffered in recent years. She previously felt pretty good about herself and the contribution she was making to her family life. Her entire world centered around her need to be the best mother and wife she could be. Somewhere along the way she lost the feeling that she could adequately fill her parental role in the home.

There was one serious flaw to this mother's well-intended plans for her family. She forgot about her own needs! At first she felt uncomfortable when I mentioned that her emotional health had an effect on her teenage children's emotions. But as we talked she realized that when her children did something wrong, she blew up at them quickly, causing their emotions to rise. When she was irritable, she was easily drawn into family conflicts. Little tiffs that she previously handled well turned into huge blowouts because she was stressed. These battles beat up her sense of confidence as a mother. Her children realized it and often took advantage of her shaken self-esteem. Having no one to anchor themselves to emotionally, the children's anger got out of hand.

When counseling parents of angry teenagers, I often suggest that the parent take time to recharge her own batteries. While advising parents to be "selfish" may seem to have little to do with controlling an angry teenager, the indirect effect of caring for personal needs has a positive effect on young people. One teenager stated, "I don't know what's gotten into my mom, but she's been a lot more active lately. She goes out with her friends more. She spends more time fixing herself up before going to work. She and Dad have even been to two movies the last couple weeks. That's something they *never* do." When asked how this affected him, the young person quickly responded, "Oh, she's a lot easier to live with. We haven't had nearly as many fights as we usually do."

Afterword

◆

As the doorbell rang, a father answered its call. As the door opened, the man was greeted by a howl, "Trick or treeeeat!" Before him were several children dressed in a ghoulish assortment of costumes intended to scare and frighten in the name of fun.

"Oh, my goodness," the man played along with their game. "You scared me with your costumes. For a minute I thought I was being invaded by a bunch of monsters!" The neighborhood guests squealed with excitement, waiting for the treat they had come to collect. After gathering their booty, they tromped off to the next house, continuing their fun.

Returning to the den, the man's wife asked, "Whose children were at the door this time?"

"I'm not quite sure who that was. I couldn't tell because they all had on masks. I think one of them was the Vickers boy, but I'm not certain."

How many of us have been through this same simple scenario? I dare say most adults have met children of uncertain identity at one time or another. We think we know who we have just talked to, but because of a mask on the child, we cannot be sure who that young person actually is.

Let's ask this same question, but add a different twist. How many of us have had encounters with a teenager who lives in the house, yet we leave our conversation unsure of whom we have just talked with? Again, all of us have had that sort of head-scratching experience with a teenager.

Like children on Halloween night, teenagers mask their anger in various ways. As we have seen, sometimes teenage anger bellows loudly, showing all its force and fury. On other occasions it seeps out of the adolescent, almost escaping detection. Misused anger can provoke the teen to become someone he is not intended to be. It also causes parents to feel helpless to bring out the good that hides deep inside every young person.

One characteristic that makes anger such a difficult emotion to manage is its ability to take on so many appearances. It is hard to believe that one emotion can pop up in so many disguises! It is the ease with which anger is masked that encourages an adolescent to misuse it. Anger can simultaneously become a communication tool and a manipulative device. On the one hand, anger may point to an unmet need in the teen's life. On the other hand, it may become a weapon to attack a seemingly unfair world.

There are times when we would like to ask a child to lift his Halloween mask so we may know his true identity. Likewise, we would like to peek beneath the masks anger wears to understand its purpose in the behavior of the adolescent. A parent's knowledge of teen anger gives that adult the opportunity to be a more effective family leader.

I view knowledge as an instrument that lets one person effectively react to the needs of another. To parent effectively requires the use of many tools. An understanding of your teenager and his unique emotional struggles puts you, as the household leader, in a position to promote (and not to hinder) your child's growth.

Teens put away their masks when they are with adults who understand them completely and respond to them lovingly. "Halloween is for kids," my teenage daughter has said. She's right. The adolescent should take off her mask and show the world her true self, angry feelings and all. The fortunate ones have their parents as a guide.

A word from Proverbs speaks aptly to parents of struggling teenagers. "Wisdom is the principal thing; Therefore get wisdom. And in all your getting, get understanding. Exalt her, and she will promote you; She will bring you honor, when you embrace her" (Prov. 4:7–8).

About the Author

◆

D r. Wm. Lee Carter is a licensed psychologist with Child Psychiatry Associates, a private practice in Waco, Texas. He provides psychological counseling and consultation to children, teens, and their families. He has spoken at conferences and seminars across the U.S.

Lee's wife, Julie, is a teacher. They have three daughters: Emily and Sarah—who are teenagers—and Mary.